WITHDRAWN

POLAND

in Pictures

Jeffrey Zuehlke

TF
CB

Twenty-First Century Books

Contents

Twenty-First Century Books
A division of Lerner Publishing Group
241 First Avenue North
Minneapolis, MN 55401 U.S.A.

Website address: www.lernerbooks.com

web enhanced @ www.vgsbooks.com

Library of Congress Cataloging-in-Publication Data

Zuehlke, Jeffrey, 1968-
    Poland in pictures / by Jeffrey Zuehlke—Rev. and expanded.
        p.   cm. — (Visual geography series)
    Includes bibliographical references and index.
    ISBN-13: 978-0-8225-2676-6 (lib. bdg. : alk. paper)
    ISBN-10: 0-8225-2676-X (lib. bdg. : alk. paper)
    1. Poland—Juvenile literature. I. Title. II. Visual geography series (Minneapolis, Minn.)
DK4040.Z84 2006
943.8—dc22
                                                        2005010520

Manufactured in the United States of America
1 2 3 4 5 6 – BP – 11 10 09 08 07 06

INTRODUCTION

On May 1, 2004, Poland, along with nine other central European nations, officially became a member of the European Union (EU), an organization that facilitates cooperation among its members in matters of trade, politics, and economics. For Poland, joining the EU was an important step in the country's long journey toward becoming a full participant in a free and democratic Europe.

Yet Poland's history as a democratic nation goes back many centuries. In the sixteenth century, a Polish-led commonwealth stretched across much of central Europe and was one of the first European kingdoms to hold elections to determine its leaders. For centuries, Poland was considered one of the most politically and culturally advanced societies in Europe.

However, Poland's more recent history has been marked by tragedy, war, and division. In the late-1700s, the country's powerful neighbors, Russia, Austria, and Prussia (part of modern-day Germany), used their superior military power to divide and eventually eliminate the nation

of Poland. The final partition of Poland in 1795 left millions of ethnic Poles under the heel of foreign rulers who sought to strip them of their language and culture. Yet the Polish people persevered and held on to their identity throughout the nineteenth century.

The violence and upheaval of World War I (1914–1918) led to a redrawing of Europe's map. Ethnic Poles seized this opportunity to resurrect their long-dead nation, and in late 1918, they established a new and independent Polish state. But Poland's triumph was short-lived. On September 1, 1939, the forces of Adolf Hitler's Nazi Germany touched off World War II (1939–1945) with a massive invasion of Poland. Soon after, armies of the Soviet Union (a large empire based in Russia) also invaded Poland, from the east. Within weeks, the conquest of Poland was complete, but the Polish peoples' suffering was only beginning.

During the war years, German and Soviet occupiers brutalized the Polish population, and Hitler's forces used several sites in Poland to

SWEDEN

BALTIC SEA

LITHUANIA

Slowinski
National Park

KALININGRAD
[RUSSIA]

Ustka
Darlowo

Gdynia
Gdansk

Gulf of
Gdansk

Czarna
Hancza
River

Malbork

Raczki
Elblaskie

Szczecin

Pomeranian Lakes

Vistula River

Masurian Lakes

Lake
Sniardwy

Oder River

Bug River

BELARUS

Gniezno

Poznan

Warta River

Warsaw

Vistula River

Lodz

Belchatow

Bug River

Nysa River

GERMANY

Wroclaw

Oder River

SILESIA

Czestochowa

San River

SUDETEN MOUNTAINS

Gliwice
Canal

Katowice

Birkenau

Krakow

Nowa Huta

CZECH REPUBLIC

Auschwitz

Oswiecim

CARPATHIAN MOUNTAINS

UKRAINE

TATRA MTNS.

Rysy Peak

BESKID MTNS.

Zakopane

Tatra
National Park

SLOVAKIA

Poland

— International border
⊛ Capital city
• City
■ Concentration camp

0 — 50 Miles
0 — 50 KM

N

ATLANTIC
OCEAN

500 Miles
500 KM

RUSSIA

POLAND

EUROPE

AFRICA

HUNGARY

carry out the Nazis' Final Solution—a plan to eliminate several European races and ethnic groups, particularly Jews—by engaging in mass executions in specially built extermination camps. Millions of Poles were murdered during this event, known as the Holocaust.

By 1945, long after the Germans and Soviets had turned against each other, the Soviet forces drove the Germans out of Poland. But Poland's hopes of reviving its independence were soon dashed when postwar agreements allowed Soviet leader Joseph Stalin to install a pro-Soviet Communist government in Poland. For the next several decades, the Polish people lived in a Communist society that guaranteed work and wages for its citizens but provided a low standard of living and virtually no freedom for political, religious, or cultural expression. Poland became a part of the Eastern Bloc—a group of Soviet-dominated countries including Hungary, Czechoslovakia, and East Germany—that challenged the democracies of Western Europe and their ally, the United States, in a decades-long political conflict known as the Cold War (1945–1991).

Under Communism, Poland was transformed from a largely agricultural nation into an industrial center that provided coal, steel, and other raw materials to the Soviet Union and other Eastern Bloc nations. The country's economy was centrally planned, meaning government officials set wages, prices, and production levels. But poor economic management eventually caused shortages of food and other consumer goods.

During the 1980s, increasing dissatisfaction with the Communist regime led to a series of strikes organized by Solidarity, an independent labor union. The strikes ignited a widespread revolt against Communism in central Europe and, in 1989, brought about a return of democracy to Poland.

Since that time, Poles have at times struggled as they work to transform from a centrally planned economy into a more open economy based on supply and demand. Yet Poland has made great strides since the 1980s, and the country remains on course for a better future.

THE LAND

Flat plains, river valleys, and gently rolling hills dominate Poland's landscape. A 277-mile (446 kilometer) coastline on the Baltic Sea in northern Europe forms the country's northern border. To the northeast is Kaliningrad, a part of Russia. To the east are Lithuania, Belarus, and Ukraine—independent republics that were once part of the Soviet Union. Rugged mountains in the south define boundaries with Slovakia and the Czech Republic. Germany is Poland's western neighbor.

Poland's total land area of 120,728 square miles (312,685 sq. km) makes it slightly smaller than the state of New Mexico. From west to east, Poland measures 430 miles (692 km). The greatest distance from north to south is 395 miles (635 km).

 Topography

Poland can be divided, from north to south, into several regions stretching across the country. In the north are the Coastal Lowlands,

a strip of beaches and lagoons along the shores of the Baltic Sea. Natural harbors exist at Gdansk and Gdynia in the north and at Szczecin in the northwest.

Farther inland, the sparsely populated Lake Region occupies much of northern Poland. Thousands of years ago, glaciers (slow-moving masses of ice) covered the plains of the area. As they retreated northward, the glaciers carved hollows that later became freshwater lakes and peat bogs (swamps filled with decayed plants). The glaciers also formed small, rocky hills known as moraines, which crisscross the land in irregular patterns. Dense forests make lumbering the most important industry in the Lake Region.

The Central Plains, which cover the middle of Poland, are part of the Great European Plain, which extends from France in the west to Russia in the east. Moraines and broad river valleys dominate these lowlands, which are intensively farmed. Warsaw, the capital of Poland, straddles the banks of the Vistula River in the eastern part of

The **Tatra Mountains** rise behind rolling fields in southern Poland.

the Central Plains. The Bialowieza Forest—one of the largest in Europe—lies northeast of Warsaw on the Belarussian border.

The rolling hills of the Polish Uplands reach about 1,000 feet (305 meters) in elevation south of the Central Plains. In the southwest, the political region of Silesia extends into the Czech Republic and Germany. It contains important industrial centers and most of Poland's mineral resources. The plateaus and hills of this area also support farms.

Polska, the country's name in the Polish language, comes from the word *polana*, meaning "clearing," or from *pole*, meaning "field."

The Carpathian Forelands cover a long, narrow territory between the Vistula and the San rivers in southeastern Poland. Rich soil supports a wide variety of crops in this region. In the southwest, the Sudeten Mountains rise to 5,000 feet (1,524 m) above sea level. Forests cover the rounded peaks of these highlands.

The Beskid and Tatra ranges, spurs of the Carpathians, line Poland's southern border. Rysy Peak, the highest point in Poland, towers 8,199 feet (2,499 m) in the Tatra Mountains.

SWEDEN

BALTIC SEA

LITHUANIA

Gulf of
Gdansk

KALININGRAD
[RUSSIA]

COASTAL LOWLANDS

L A K E

Raczki
Elblaskie

R E G I O N

Czarna
Hancza
River

Masurian Lakes

Lake
Sniardwy

Pomeranian Lakes

Tuchola
Forest

Vistula River

Bialowieza
Forest

Oder River

Bug River

BELARUS

Warta River

C E N T R A L   P L A I N S

Vistula River

GERMANY

Nysa River

Oder River

P O L I S H   U P L A N D S

Bug River

CZECH REPUBLIC

SUDETEN MOUNTAINS

CARPATHIAN FORELANDS

San River

C A R P A T H I A N   M O U N T A I N S

UKRAINE

TATRA MTNS.

BESKID MTNS.

Rysy Peak

SLOVAKIA

Poland

Feet	Meters	
9843	3000	Mountains
6582	2000	Uplands
3281	1000	Lowlands
1640	500	

Elevation

N

——— International border
▲ Mountain peak

0   100 Miles
0   100 KM

HUNGARY

0   500 Miles
0   500 KM

ATLANTIC
OCEAN

RUSSIA

POLAND

E U R O P E

AFRICA

Rivers and Lakes

For centuries, navigable rivers and canals (human-made waterways) have provided Poland with an important shipping network. This system also links Poland with foreign countries through seaports on the Baltic coast.

Poland's longest river, the Vistula, begins in the Tatra Mountains. Navigable over much of its course, the Vistula flows 670 miles (1,078 km) northward through central Poland before emptying into the Gulf of Gdansk. The Bug River, which feeds into the Vistula, forms part of Poland's boundary with Ukraine and Belarus. Several other rivers flow westward into the Vistula from outside Poland's borders.

The Oder and the Nysa rivers follow Poland's western boundary with Germany. The Oder begins in the mountains of Slovakia, flows northwestward, and ends at a wide lagoon on the Baltic Sea north of Szczecin. Feeding the Oder are the Warta River and several small streams in central and western Poland.

Rivers, streams, and canals connect thousands of lakes in the plains and forests of Poland's Lake Region. The Masurain Lakes in the northeast and the Pomeranian Lakes in the northwest are popular spots for camping, fishing, and water sports. Lake Sniardwy, the country's largest lake, covers 36 square miles (93 sq. km). Smaller lakes exist in Poland's mountainous regions, where glaciers carved shallow basins between the steep slopes.

Climate

Poland's weather varies greatly, depending on each region's elevation and distance from the seacoast. Mild ocean winds bring cool summers and moderate winters to the Baltic shore, where temperatures average 31°F (0°C) in January, the coldest month, and 63°F (17°C) in July, the warmest month. Warm sea currents allow the harbor of Gdansk to remain ice free all year.

Interior regions of Poland have slightly colder winters and warmer summers. In Warsaw the average temperature is 27°F (–3°C) in January and 67°F (19°C) in July. Temperatures are lowest in the mountains of the south, which have the country's highest elevations. The *halny*, a dry wind, occasionally blows from the south, moderating the cold temperatures of this area.

Frequent showers and thunderstorms interrupt Poland's cool summer days. Annual precipitation averages 24 inches (61 centimeters) on the plains, while certain areas of the Carpathian Mountains receive 60 inches (152 cm) or more of rain and snow a year. Snow covers the Carpathians for one to three months during the winter.

Flora and Fauna

Industrial pollution and natural diseases have damaged many of Poland's forests, which cover about one-fourth of the country's land. The Bialowieza Forest, the only unharvested forest in central Europe, lies 160 miles (247 km) east of Warsaw. Stands of yew and mountain ash trees flourish in the Tuchola Forest, which stretches from the Vistula River westward to the lakes of north central Poland.

Large tracts of timber in the north and in the Carpathian Mountains supply Poland's lumber industry. About 75 percent of these trees are evergreens, such as pine, spruce, and fir. Deciduous (leaf-shedding) trees—including ash, poplar, willow, birch, beech, elm, oak, and alder—are common in the Lake Region, in the Central Plains, and in the south.

Poland's national parks shelter a wide variety of uncommon plants. Visitors to Tatra National Park can see rare stone pine and edelweiss, a small flowering herb that grows at high elevations. Cheddar pink and tormentil flowers grow in the forests of the Lake Region, and the martagon lily thrives in the south-ern mountains.

Although Poles have cleared vast tracts of forested land and destroyed much natural habitat, wildlife has survived in several regions. The Bialowieza Forest is home to bison, elks, lynxes, bears, and foxes. Wild boars, wolves, and mountain deer roam the valleys and forests of the Carpathian Mountains. The Polish government officially protects the wild swans, cormorants, and black storks that inhabit the lakes and rivers of the north.

Despite severe river and coastal pollution from cities and industries,

THE BISON

The European bison is Europe's largest mammal—the biggest bison can weigh up to 2,700 pounds (1,000 kilograms). Yet, despite their size, these scruffy looking cattle can run as fast as 30 miles per hour (50 km/hr). Centuries ago, hundreds of thousands of bison roamed the plains and forests of Europe, but the population dwindled rapidly as human settlement steadily shrank their habitat. By the early twentieth century, the species was extinct in the wild—only a few dozen remained in zoos throughout the world.

In 1929 animal conservationists began to reintroduce bison into the Bialowieza Forest. The program proved successful and led to reintroductions of bison into other parts of Europe. About 2,500 European bison exist in the wild.

This **bison** roams the snowy Bialowieza Forest in eastern Poland. Visit www.vgsbooks.com for links to sites with more photos of Poland's wildlife.

nearly fifty species of fish have survived in Poland. The most common are pike, trout, salmon, miller's-thumb, whitefish, eel, and crayfish. Commercial fishers harvest herring and cod from the Baltic Sea.

Natural Resources and Environmental Issues

Silesia and the Polish Uplands contain most of the country's mineral wealth. Poland's chief natural resource is coal, an essential fuel for energy production and industry. Most of the country's reserves are in southwestern and central Poland, including one of the world's largest coal fields near the southern city of Katowice.

In the 1950s, engineers discovered vast copper deposits in western Poland. Copper and coal have since become the country's main mineral exports. Workers also mine deposits of sulfur, iron ore, lead, and zinc.

Rock salt deposits in southern and central Poland are among the world's largest. A gigantic mine at Wieliczka, near Krakow, has produced salt for many centuries. Deposits of amber (fossilized tree resin)—a material used in jewelry making—exist on the Baltic seacoast. Poland taps small fields of oil and natural gas in the foothills of the Carpathian Mountains.

Poland's natural environment experienced severe damage under Communism. In its push to develop and maximize heavy industries such as coal mines and steel plants, the Communist government showed little regard for the country's environment. As a result, Poland was one of the most polluted countries in Europe by the late 1980s.

Since the end of Communism in 1989, the Polish government has worked hard to improve the country's environment and has achieved very good results. Scientific studies show that Poland has reduced its industrial and agricultural water pollution by half and significantly reduced its industrial air pollution. These successes are due to a variety

THE BLACK TRIANGLE

During the 1980s, the heavily industrialized Katowice district in southern Poland was one of the most polluted areas in Europe. Katowice, part of the historical region known as Silesia, contributed about 20 to 25 percent of the country's air pollution emissions, while only covering about 2 percent of Poland's land area.

Katowice combined with parts of neighboring Communist states East Germany and Czechoslovakia to form what came to be known as the Black Triangle. Rivers in this area were polluted by industrial waste. Some valleys were plagued with constant smog. Acid rain destroyed many mountain forests and acidified soil. These conditions led to significant increases in chronic respiratory disorders such as lung disease and emphysema. Since the end of Communism, the Polish government has made great strides in cleaning up this region.

Acid rain has devastated these spruce trees in a national park in southwestern Poland.

of factors, including closing many inefficient, polluting factories, and upgrading numerous factories with more environmentally friendly equipment. In addition, the Polish government has also passed strict antipollution laws that require industries to make environmental protection a high priority.

Cities

World War II devastated the people and cities of Poland. Wartime deaths, emigration, and forced resettlement reduced the country's population by about one-third. After the war, many farmers abandoned their rural villages and sought jobs in Poland's cities, where a rapid program of rebuilding and industrialization created new homes and jobs.

About 60 percent of Poland's 38.6 million people live in cities. Many large urban centers lie within a vast industrial and mining zone in the Polish Uplands. Smaller towns and cities dot the Central Plains, while the Baltic coast region includes several major port cities.

Warsaw is the capital of Poland and its largest city.

WARSAW Warsaw grew along the banks of the Vistula River in east central Poland. Home to 1.7 million people, the city has been a trading hub since the fifteenth century and the capital of Poland since 1596. Warsaw experienced war and occupation in the eighteenth and nineteenth centuries, as stronger European states fought over Polish territory.

During World War II, aerial bombing and street fighting destroyed 90 percent of the buildings in Warsaw, and the city's population fell from more than 1 million to 160,000. The Poles later used old photos and drawings as a guide to rebuild Stare Miasto (Old Town), the capital's medieval center. Engineers and architects reconstructed houses, palaces, churches, and a royal castle. Contrasting sharply with Stare Miasto are the modern stores, offices, and high-rise apartments of the downtown Centrum complex. The Palace of Culture and Science, a skyscraper built under Poland's Communist regime, towers over the city.

An important transportation hub, Warsaw is also an industrial center that produces steel, cars, chemicals, textiles, and beer. Students attend several major universities in the city. Long a lively cultural center, Warsaw boasts museums, libraries, theaters, and concert halls.

Secondary Cities

The city of Lodz (population 840,000), in central Poland, has thrived from textile production for more than a century. Hundreds of textile mills operate alongside chemical and metallurgical factories. The city is also known as the Polish Hollywood—it is home to a renowned film school and a number of motion picture studios.

Poland's oldest city, Krakow (population 770,000) lies along the Vistula about 150 miles (241 km) south of Warsaw. Founded about A.D. 70, Krakow later became a commercial and political center. It was Poland's capital city from the early fourteenth century until 1596. Jagiellonian University, the country's oldest university, was founded in Krakow in 1364.

SCHINDLER'S LIST

U.S. film director Steven Spielberg shot much of his famous Holocaust story *Schindler's List* (1993) in Krakow. The powerful movie tells the true story of Oskar Schindler, a Czech-born Nazi factory owner who uses Jewish slave laborers in his Krakow factory. When Schindler realizes that the Nazis plan to wipe out the city's entire Jewish population, he resolves to save as many people as he can. In the end, he succeeded in saving about 1,100 Jews from extermination.

The **Wawel Cathedral** is one of the most notable pieces of architecture in Krakow. It is one of the city's main tourist attractions.

Poland's rulers were crowned in Krakow's fourteenth-century Wawel Cathedral, which contains the tombs of many famous Poles. Market Square, lined by palaces and old mansions, is a traditional setting for festivals and national celebrations. The German army made the city its occupation headquarters during World War II and spared many of Krakow's ancient buildings from destruction.

Modern Krakow is a trading center for minerals, agricultural products, and timber. The massive iron and steelworks in the suburb Nowa Huta make the surrounding region one of Poland's principal manufacturing areas. Factories within Krakow furnish building materials, machinery, and chemicals.

Wroclaw (population 675,000) lies on the Oder River about 200 miles (322 km) southwest of Warsaw. A railroad and industrial center, Wroclaw was for centuries the capital of the German-speaking region of Lower Silesia. A hub of Poland's electronics and computer industries, Wroclaw is also a leading producer of railcars. A network of canals and tributaries crosses Wroclaw and its surrounding region, and Poles have nicknamed Wroclaw the City of Bridges.

This **medieval crane** is located in historic Gdansk. Gdansk has been an important Polish seaport for hundreds of years.

Poland's major seaports, including Gdynia, Gdansk, and Szczecin, lie near natural lagoons and gulfs on the Baltic coast. Gdansk (population 475,000), on the Gulf of Gdansk, began as a fishing village in the late 900s and has been a major port since the 1500s. In 1980 workers in the Lenin shipyards formed the Solidarity union, the first independent labor organization in any Communist nation.

Visit www.vgsbooks.com for links to websites with additional information about the many things to see and do in Poland's cities, as well as for links to websites about Poland's weather, natural resources, plants and animals, and more.

HISTORY AND GOVERNMENT

Archaeologists believe that humans have lived in Poland for at least 200,000 years, but very little is known about the region's earliest inhabitants. Prehistoric peoples first settled communities in Poland's river valleys about 15,000 years ago. In the first century A.D., ethnic Slavs from the east moved into the lowlands of central and northern Poland.

The Polanie (plain dwellers), a Slavic group, built small towns called *grody* in the region of the Warta River. Because Poland's lowlands and plains offered little protection from attack, the Polanie constructed strong wooden walls around their settlements. Outside the walls, the Polanie cleared land to raise grain and livestock. The people of the grody traded their goods and handicrafts with other Slavic groups inhabiting central Europe.

For several centuries, the Slavs remained untouched by events in western Europe. Armies of the Roman Empire, which was based in Italy, had conquered much of Europe by A.D. 100. Although a road linked Poland's Baltic coast with Roman towns to the south, the empire never subdued Slavic peoples in eastern Europe. Nor did early Roman Catholic missionaries, who spread the Christian faith to Germany, succeed in gaining converts among the Polanie.

As the population of Poland increased, the Slavic peoples divided into groups, and some groups migrated from the area. Between 200 and 500, the Eastern Slavs moved to the areas that would become Belarus, Ukraine, and Russia. The Western Slavs, a group that included the Polanie, inhabited the territory of Poland as well as the future lands of the Czechs and the Slovaks to the south.

The Piast Dynasty

The Polanie, who lived in about twenty independent communities, built new towns in the basins of the Vistula and Oder rivers. Large, organized Polanie states arose in the south near Krakow and in the west near Poznan. Trading centers also developed along the Baltic seacoast.

The Polanie built fortified castles to protect their land from the attacks of German Catholic crusaders (religious warriors), who sought to convert the Slavic peoples to Christianity by force.

To resist these invasions, the Polanie united in the mid-ninth century under Piast, a ruler celebrated in Polish tales and legends. By the tenth century, the members of the Piast dynasty (family of rulers) were bringing the people of the plains, the Lake Region, and the Baltic coast under their control. In 966 Prince Mieszko I established the capital of the Piast state at Gniezno, near the modern-day city of Poznan.

To strengthen his realm's defenses and to stop the attacks of German crusaders, Mieszko allied with the Holy Roman Empire, a confederation of states in central Europe. Prince Mieszko also formed an alliance with Bohemia, a Slavic state to the south, by marrying a Bohemian princess. In 966 Mieszko converted to Roman Catholicism, the faith of his new wife, and invited Catholic missionaries to Poland. In 1025 the pope—the Catholic Church leader—officially recognized the Polish realm by crowning Boleslaus I, Mieszko's son and successor. The Poles adopted the Latin alphabet, used by the Roman Catholic Church, to write their Slavic language.

> At the height of Mieszko I's rule, his lands covered about 96,500 square miles (250,000 sq. km) and were inhabited by about 1.2 million people.

A brave and ambitious ruler, King Boleslaus conquered land in Germany and extended his realm as far east as the Dnieper River, which flows southward through Ukraine and empties into the Black Sea. Trade along the Dnieper linked Poland with Black Sea ports and helped the Polish kingdom prosper.

At the same time, a dispute among church leaders was dividing Christianity into two factions. This led to the founding of the Eastern Orthodox Church in the eleventh century. Orthodox Christianity was centered in the city of Constantinople (modern Istanbul, Turkey). Although many eastern European Slavs became Orthodox Christians, the people of Poland and Bohemia were allied with the pope and remained within the Roman Catholic Church, which remained centered in Rome, Italy.

◉ Decline and Invasion

Poland experienced violent internal conflicts after the death of Boleslaus I in 1025. When Boleslaus II disputed with the Polish nobility (wealthy landowners), the Catholic bishop of Krakow,

Stanislaw, took the side of the nobles. In 1079 Boleslaus ordered the murder of the bishop, an action that led the pope to impose sanctions (penalties) on Poland.

The Poles were also fighting with their German neighbors. In the early 1100s, Boleslaus III battled the forces of the Holy Roman Empire for control of Pomerania (northwestern Poland). But he weakened Poland by decreeing that his kingdom would be divided equally among his sons. During the next two centuries, this system of inheritance created many small, semi-independent principalities (realms of princes). Rivalries among the Polish nobles and princes left the Polish people disorganized and powerless to defend their long frontiers.

Poland's neighbors took advantage of the growing chaos within the kingdom. The Order of the Teutonic Knights, an organization of Catholic warriors, attacked from the north. Lithuania, a nation on the Baltic Sea to the northeast, also invaded Polish lands. In 1240 a huge force of Mongolian Tartars advanced from their base in eastern Asia to devastate Poland and much of eastern Europe.

After the Tartars retreated from Europe, Poland began a slow recovery. German artisans and merchants settled in Polish towns and ports. Poland also welcomed large numbers of Jews who were fleeing persecution in other European nations. Membership in the Hanseatic League—a commercial union of northern European cities—allowed trade to flourish in Krakow, Gdansk, and other cities of the kingdom.

The **Malbork Castle** was built in the city of Malbork by the Teutonic Knights starting in 1275. It is a classic example of a medieval fortress. For links to sites where you can learn more about Poland's history, visit www.vgsbooks.com.

Casimir the Great and the Jagiellonian Dynasty

After the assassination of the Polish king Przemysl II in 1295, a dispute erupted over the succession to the throne. The king of Bohemia, Wenceslaus II, sought to extend his power in the region by attacking Polish territory. After the death of Wenceslaus in 1305, a member of the Piast dynasty gained support from the pope and was crowned King Ladislas I in 1320. Following his coronation in Krakow, Ladislas made the city the new Polish capital.

Poland was still a weak and divided nation when Ladislas's son Casimir III, began ruling in 1333. By strengthening the monarchy's control over Poland, Casimir ended internal conflicts and reunified the nation, earning the title Casimir the Great. He also secured Poland's borders by forming alliances with Lithuania and with Hungary, a powerful kingdom to the south.

Casimir made many important internal reforms. The king reorganized Poland's laws and administration. He also established laws to protect the rights of the Polish peasants (rural farm laborers). A patron of education, Casimir founded the nation's first university at Krakow, in 1364.

After Casimir died in 1370 without an heir, his nephew King Ludwig of Hungary took the throne. Jadwiga, the daughter of Ludwig, became Poland's queen in 1382. Four years later, Jadwiga married the Lithuanian duke Jogaila. The Polish nobles, who sought Lithuania's help in battling the Teutonic Knights, elected Jogaila as King Wladislaw II Jagiello in 1386. Although Poland and Lithuania still had separate governments, the two nations were ruled by the Jagiellonian dynasty.

CASIMIR THE GREAT

Casimir III was the only Polish monarch to earn the title the Great. In addition to reforming Poland's laws and promoting education, Casimir also helped strengthen his kingdom's defenses by building fifty castles throughout his realm and building stone walls around thirty key Polish cities. An old saying about Casimir states, "He found Poland made of wood and left it made of stone."

Casimir also established and fostered the development of new cities in several important locations and oversaw the building of numerous fisheries, granaries, and mills, all of which spurred economic development. Casimir furthered the country's economic growth by introducing a stable currency that allowed freer trade both domestically and across his kingdom's borders.

The Jagiellonian rulers scored several decisive military victories during the fifteenth century. In 1410 an army of Poles and Lithuanians defeated the Teutonic Knights at the Battle of Tannenberg. After losing several more battles to Wladislaw's successor, Casimir IV, the Teutonic Knights agreed to the Peace of Thorn and gave up lands in Prussia (northeastern Germany) to Poland.

After the signing of the Peace of Thorn, Poland reached the height of its power and influence in central Europe. Under Jagiellonian rule, the kingdom also made important economic, political, and cultural advances. Printers produced the first Polish books during this period. Poland's scholars founded new universities and began to use Polish instead of Latin, the traditional language of religion and scholarship in Europe. The Polish astronomer Mikolaj Kopernik, also known by his Latin name Copernicus, made important discoveries that laid the foundation for modern astronomy.

While these changes were in progress, the Christian faith was in turmoil. A revolt against the Catholic Church erupted in Germany, where the teachings of Martin Luther sparked the Protestant Reformation. Protestant churches—which did not recognize the authority of the Catholic pope—were founded in several northern European countries. The Scandinavian kingdom of Sweden, across the Baltic Sea from Poland, became a Protestant realm. Although it remained a Catholic nation, Poland allowed members of other faiths to worship freely. Poland became a center of Jewish culture, and its Jewish community became one of the largest in the world.

The Polish Parliament and Foreign Rule

During the reign of Casimir IV, a class of warriors and landowners called the *szlachta* increased its control over Poland's land and peasant farmers. High taxes on the peasants forced many of them to become serfs—rural workers who were bound to the estates of the landowners.

The growing power of the upper classes had allowed them to form a national parliament (lawmaking body) in 1493. This legislature included a senate of wealthy nobles and a Sejm, or lower house, of landowners. In 1505 the parliament wrote the nation's first constitution, which stated that the Polish kings could pass no new laws without the parliament's consent. The Sejm also gave itself the power to vote approval of each king.

In 1569 Poland and Lithuania formally united under Polish authority. After the unification, Poland's kings ruled a huge realm that included Germans, Poles, Lithuanians, and Ukrainians.

Zygmunt II Augustus, the last Jagiellonian ruler, died in 1572, ending the Jagiellonian dynasty.

After Zygmunt's death, the Polish nobles increased their power by assuming the right to elect future kings. This led to intense rivalries within Poland, which the parliament tried to calm by electing foreign princes to the Polish throne. In 1575 the parliament elected as king Stephen Bathory, a Hungarian prince. A strong military leader, Bathory defeated an invasion of Poland ordered by the czar (emperor) of Russia, Ivan IV.

Zygmunt III Vasa, a Swedish prince, succeeded Bathory in 1586. Vasa was the first of several Swedes to become king of Poland. But this arrangement eventually caused a religious war between Protestant Sweden and Catholic Poland. Swedish forces invaded Poland in 1655, burning and looting towns and farms.

The Poles stopped this invasion, but many years of military conflict and economic decline followed. The Cossacks, a group of free peasants who lived in areas of Ukraine and Russia, had seized Polish territory before the Swedish invasion. Fierce and capable soldiers, the Cossacks recognized no outside authority. They brought into their ranks many Ukrainian peasants opposed to Polish rule. As Polish authority weakened, the growing Russian Empire was able to seize large sections of eastern Poland.

Another threat came from the Ottoman Turks, who had conquered Constantinople and much of eastern Europe from their base in Asia Minor (modern Turkey). In 1683 Jan Sobieski—who had been elected King Jan III of Poland in the previous decade—defeated the Turks at Vienna, Austria. His victory stopped the Turkish advance across Europe.

Jan Sobieski was a Polish-born military hero. He was elected king in 1674.

The Partitions of Poland

Despite Sobieski's triumph, conflict within the Polish parliament shook the kingdom. Under King Augustus II, a German who had succeeded Jan Sobieski, Poland began to lose its independence to its stronger neighbors. When Augustus died in 1733, the representatives of the Russian czar bribed a large faction of the Sejm to elect Augustus's son.

At the same time, heavy taxes were creating a drain on Polish agriculture and trade. Poland's military declined, leaving the kingdom defenseless against foreign armies. The nobility did little to unite Poland's rival political factions and weakened the realm through their incompetence and corruption. In addition, the Sejm had adopted the Liberum Veto. Under this system, any single member of parliament could veto—or stop—new laws from being passed.

The Liberum Veto led to governmental chaos, which gave Poland's enemies an opportunity to capture Polish territory. In 1772 Prussia and Austria—two strong realms to the west and south, respectively—joined with Russia in annexing (seizing) nearly one-third of Poland's land. This was the first of three partitions of Poland.

In the years following the first partition, a movement for governmental reform gathered force in the Polish parliament. Despite the opposition of many Polish nobles, the legislature adopted a new constitution in 1791. This document reduced the Sejm's power by abolishing the Liberum Veto and by making the crown hereditary instead of elective. The new constitution also guaranteed the legal rights of all citizens.

The Russian czarina (empress), Catherine II, did not want her own citizens demanding such reforms, however. With the cooperation of several Polish nobles, she ordered the invasion and seizure of eastern Poland. At the same time, the Prussians took some western land and the port of Gdansk.

This second partition of Poland inspired a revolt led by the Polish patriot Tadeusz Kosciuszko. In 1794 Kosciuszko defeated a Russian army at Warsaw, but the combined forces of Russia and Prussia outnumbered the Poles. In the following year, Russia, Prussia, and Austria crushed Kosciuszko's revolt and forced the Polish king to abdicate. The three empires divided the remaining Polish territory among themselves, and the kingdom of Poland ceased to exist.

Foreign Rule and World War I

Following the third partition, many Polish soldiers and politicians emigrated to France, where a popular revolution had toppled the

French monarchy. Polish military leaders formed fighting units in France in the hope of one day liberating their nation. Under the French general Napoleon Bonaparte, these units fought with the French army against Austria and Prussia. After defeating Prussia in 1807, Napoleon established the Grand Duchy of Warsaw, a democratic state under French administration.

A coalition of several nations defeated Napoleon in 1815 and founded the small Kingdom of Poland under Russian control. Polish lands annexed by the Grand Duchy were returned to Prussia and Austria. During the reign of the Russian czar Alexander I, the Kingdom of Poland gained a new constitution and made important advances in industry and education.

Yet the Polish people demanded complete independence. When a rebellion broke out in 1830, the czar reacted by incorporating eastern Poland into the Russian Empire. Russia abolished the Polish constitution and parliament and seized control of Poland's economy. By the 1860s, Russian had become the language of administration and education in what had once been Poland.

Foreign rule in western Poland was even stricter. In the 1870s, the Prussian leader Otto von Bismarck, who united several German-speaking states into the German Empire, tried to eliminate Polish culture in the lands under his control. The German government closed Polish Catholic schools, restricted the activities of the Catholic Church, and forced Poles in Pomerania and Silesia to use the German language. Western Poland benefited, however, from Germany's own industrial development, which included the construction of a modern railroad system.

Although they had lost their independence, Poles clung to their national identity. Violent uprisings against Russian rule inspired sympathy among many European leaders and helped Polish patriotism remain strong. Polish writers, artists, and musicians glorified their vanished nation and kept their culture alive by drawing on Polish folk and religious traditions.

By the early twentieth century, the nations of Europe had formed two strong alliances to balance the continent's rival powers. Britain sided with France and Russia to oppose Germany, Austria, and the Ottoman Empire. The Poles joined new political parties that sought the support of the European powers. Under the politician Roman Dmowski, the National Democratic Party formed ties with Russia. The Polish Socialist Party and its leader Jozef Pilsudski allied with Austria.

In the summer of 1914, World War I broke out between the two European alliances. Poland became a battleground for the armies of

Austria, Germany, and Russia. A series of defeats eventually forced the Russians to sign a peace treaty with Germany in March 1918. Later that year, however, Germany and Austria surrendered, and World War I came to an end.

The Republic of Poland

During the war, revolutionaries known as Communists had overthrown the Russian government. After withdrawing from World War I, the Russian Communist regime recognized the right of the Poles to choose their own form of government. As the war ended, a provisional (temporary) Polish government founded the independent Republic of Poland. Jozef Pilsudski, a military hero, became Poland's chief of state.

The postwar Treaty of Versailles disarmed Germany and set new borders in northern and Central Europe. The agreement granted Poland territory from Germany as well as a strip of land along the Vistula River as far as the Baltic Sea coast. Gdansk, whose population was mostly German speaking, became the free city of Danzig. The treaty placed the city under the administration of an international association known as the League of Nations.

Pilsudski's goal was to reestablish the frontiers of Poland as they had existed before the partitions. This policy brought Poland into conflict with Russia, where Communists were fighting the supporters of czarist rule. In 1920 Russia and Poland skirmished along their border. Taking advantage of the chaos within Russia, the Poles seized land beyond their own eastern frontier. In 1921 Poland and Russia finally signed a peace treaty.

The Russian Communists eventually defeated their czarist opponents and, in 1922, founded the Union of Soviet Socialist Republics (USSR). In the same year, Poland's legislature drafted a new constitution, and Pilsudski resigned as Poland's chief of state.

During the 1920s, the reestablished Sejm passed reforms in education, labor laws, and landownership. Industrial workers formed trade unions, and peasants in the countryside gained private land for raising crops. To help Polish trade, the government built a new port on the Baltic Sea at Gdynia.

Although Polish leaders were successfully rebuilding Poland, competing political factions weakened the government. In addition, opposition to Polish rule by ethnic Ukrainians, Germans, and Belarussians, as well as rising prices and widespread unemployment, caused a political crisis. By 1926 the ongoing problems had paralyzed the government.

Disappointed by the failures of Poland's legislature—and backed by the military—Pilsudski returned in 1926 and overthrew the

Polish government. He limited the powers of the Sejm and appointed a close ally as prime minister. During the late 1920s and early 1930s, Pilsudski commanded the armed forces and ruled Poland as a dictator.

New threats to Polish security arose during the 1930s. In Germany the Nazi regime of Adolf Hitler came to power and quickly began to rearm. In 1938 Hitler seized part of Czechoslovakia, which had been established south of Poland after World War I. Hitler also demanded the return of Danzig to German control.

To the east, the Soviet leader Joseph Stalin claimed eastern Poland as Soviet territory. In the summer of 1939, Hitler and Stalin signed a secret agreement—the Molotov-Ribbentrop Pact—to invade and divide Poland. As Poland rejected Hitler's demands, Britain and France pledged to help Poland in the event of a German attack.

STANDING UP TO HITLER

By the late 1930s, Poland was under increasing pressure from Adolf Hitler *(right)*, leader of Germany, to give up portions of its territory to avoid war. In a famous speech on May 5, 1939, Polish foreign minister Jozef Beck refused to back down from Hitler's intimidation:

"We in Poland do not understand the concept of peace at any price. There is only one thing in the life of people, nations, and states which is priceless, and that thing is honour."

—quoted in
An Illustrated History of Poland

World War II

On September 1, 1939, German armies staged a massive invasion of Poland. Weeks later, the forces of the Soviet Union attacked from the east. Britain and France declared war on Germany, but they did little to stop German and Soviet forces from overrunning Poland. As Warsaw fell, Polish politicians escaped to Britain to form a government-in-exile and many Polish soldiers, sailors, and pilots joined the British armed forces to fight Germany.

The German occupation of Polish cities caused massive damage. Bombing and ground fighting destroyed Danzig, Warsaw, and several other industrial centers. As World War II continued, the Nazis built concentration camps in Poland where millions of political prisoners and ethnic minorities were put to death during the Holocaust. More than three million Polish Jews lost their lives in the Holocaust.

THE HOLOCAUST

In his book, *Heart of Europe: The Past in Poland's Present*, historian Norman Davies describes the procedures used by Nazi Germany to destroy Poland's Jewish population:

"The Jewish community, which had been isolated in the ghettos for a couple of years [since the German invasion in 1939], was already wasting away from disease, malnutrition, and starvation. Now it was to be crowded into cattle-wagons, street by street, town by town, and sent to the gas chambers [in concentration camps such as Auschwitz and Birkenau]. It took only twenty minutes between the arrival of a train load to be undressed and 'disinfected' [killed] and the arrival of special detachments to strip the corpses of hair, gold fillings, and personal jewelry. . . . Hair mattresses, bone fertilizer, and soap from human fat were delivered to German industry. . . ."

Long lines of **Polish men and women** trudge toward a German concentration camp outside Warsaw during World War II.

Chiune Sugihara was one of many brave people who risked their lives and safety to save Polish Jews from the Holocaust. As an official of the Japanese government working in Lithuania, he went against his government's orders to forge thousands of documents that allowed more than six thousand Polish Jews to flee from German-occupied Poland through Lithuania.

After Hitler attacked the Soviet Union in 1941, German armies occupied all of Poland. By 1944, however, a Soviet counterattack was forcing the Germans to retreat. The Soviets soon occupied Poland, and with Soviet forces marching through the German capital of Berlin, the Nazi government finally surrendered in May 1945.

During the war, the United States and Britain recognized the members of the Polish government-in-exile as the official leaders of Poland. After the war, however, the exiles were challenged by the Committee of National Liberation, an organization dominated by Polish Communists. With his army occupying Poland, Stalin was able to force the election of Communists to important government posts. Unable to challenge Stalin or the Committee of National Liberation, the leaders of the government-in-exile did not return home.

Visit www.vgsbooks.com for links to websites with additional information about the Polish government and history, including more information about World War II and the Holocaust.

⊙ Poland under Communism

The USSR, Britain, and the United States agreed on Poland's new boundaries in 1945. The Soviet Union annexed 70,000 square miles (181,300 sq. km) from Poland's eastern area, and 40,000 square miles (103,600 sq. km) of German territory were added to western Poland. The border changes forced eight million Germans to flee northern and western Poland.

After the war, the Polish Communists organized the Polish United Workers' Party, a group modeled on the Communist Party of the Soviet Union. The Polish United Workers' Party founded trade unions and set up committees to administer cities and provinces. In 1947 the party fixed elections to bring about a Communist majority in the Polish parliament. Communist leaders later renamed their country the People's Republic of Poland.

The Polish government eventually put all private businesses under state control. Government planners set prices for goods and wages for workers. Farmers were forced to join agricultural collectives, on which the planting, harvesting, and sale of crops were under state direction. The government seized church lands, arrested critics of the regime, and forced opposition parties to reorganize under Communist control.

Poland became part of a Communist bloc of nations in central Europe. Trade and industry in Eastern Bloc countries were closely tied to the Soviet economy. The Polish government, for example, built new factories to produce heavy machinery and other industrial goods for export to the Soviet Union. The leaders of the Soviet regime exercised control over Poland's economy and political life, and Polish Communists who objected to Soviet influence lost their positions. In 1948 the government imprisoned Wladyslaw Gomulka, a Polish Communist leader, for publicly disagreeing with Soviet policy.

Polish students, artists, and workers still resisted the regime, and in 1956 violent antigovernment riots broke out in Poznan. In response, the Polish government released Gomulka, who became the first secretary (head) of the Polish Communist Party.

Gomulka freed imprisoned Catholic clergy, returned most collectivized land to private farmers, and increased contact with Western Europe. Throughout the 1960s, however, Gomulka followed most of the policies set by the Soviet leadership. Opposition to Communism continued within Poland. After widespread rioting erupted in 1970 over poor economic conditions, the party forced Gomulka to resign.

The new premier, Edward Gierek, planned to further Poland's industrialization with huge loans from Western European nations. Despite his efforts, the country's economy continued to decline. Poor harvests affected the supply of food, and in 1976 the government tried to balance its budget by increasing food prices. Violent street demonstrations quickly forced the regime to back down.

The Solidarity Movement and the End of Communism

By 1980 the Poles were suffering serious shortages of food, consumer goods, and electrical power. In the summer, workers at the Lenin Shipyards in Gdansk protested conditions by walking off the job. Workers in other Polish cities followed, and a three-week strike paralyzed the country. The government eventually agreed to most of the workers' demands, including wage increases and the right to organize unions independent of Communist control. The successful strike led to the founding of Solidarity, a national labor union headed by Lech Walesa, a shipyard electrician and strike organizer.

The rights gained by Polish workers put pressure on the government to enact other reforms. Gierek released political prisoners and lessened central control over the country's newspapers and other media. But the other Soviet and Polish Communist leaders opposed these changes. The Poles feared military intervention or an overthrow of their government by the Soviet Union. In 1981 Gierek resigned and was replaced by Wojciech Jaruzelski, a strict Communist.

Jaruzelski outlawed Solidarity and ordered Walesa's arrest. Nevertheless, demonstrations against government policies continued, and Walesa again became Solidarity's leader after his release in 1983. In addition, the labor movement found strong support among the clergy of the Roman Catholic Church. The head of the church, Pope John Paul II, was a Pole who called on Poland's Communist Party to make reforms.

Walesa organized more protests in Gdansk in 1988. Facing mounting economic problems, the government agreed to legalize Solidarity and to end one-party rule. In June 1989, non-Communist candidates, many of them from Solidarity, won election to the legislature. The parliament then chose Jaruzelski as president and Tadeusz Mazowiecki as the prime minister. A Solidarity leader, Mazowiecki headed a coalition government that included Communist and non-Communist parties.

Lech Walesa won the Nobel Peace Prize in 1983 for his efforts to bring about social change in Poland. He was later elected president.

Post-Communist Poland

In January 1990, the leaders of the Polish Communist Party renamed their organization Social Democracy of the Republic of Poland. The new government instituted a series of measures, which became known as Shock Therapy, to transform the country from a Communist state to a democracy with a free market economy. The government began selling state-owned companies to private investors—a process called privatization. As the nations of central and Eastern Europe turned away from Communism, Poland's newly privatized companies began doing business in Western Europe.

While these changes provided an economic boost, they also caused hardship. Newly privatized companies, seeking to improve efficiency and increase revenue, laid off many workers. While some Poles benefited, others struggled with unemployment—a major change from Communism, under which virtually all citizens were guaranteed a job.

After Walesa announced his candidacy for president in the fall of 1990, Jaruzelski resigned. The election then became a three-way race between Walesa, Mazowiecki, and Stanislaw Tyminski, a Polish-born businessman from Canada. When Walesa emerged as the victor in December 1990, Mazowiecki resigned as prime minister. Waldemar Pawlak, a leader of the Polish Peasants Party, became prime minister in 1993.

Walesa's presidency was marked by disputes over how the country should continue its economic reforms. These battles led to a series of government collapses and resignations. The constant changes in government and the economic hardship suffered by many Poles led to voter apathy and cynicism. Turnout for elections in the mid-1990s dropped to only 53 percent. Hardship also drove many Poles to vote for the reformed Communist Party, and in 1995 Aleksander Kwasniewski, a former Communist, narrowly defeated Walesa in the presidential election. The former Communists soon proved unpopular with the public and lost their majority in the Sejm two years later, though Kwasniewski was reelected as president in 2000.

CYNICISM IN POLITICS

The end of Communism did not succeed in giving Poles confidence in their elected leaders. In an informal poll by *The Economist* magazine, a group of Warsaw college students did not name a single contemporary Polish politician when asked to list their political role models. Instead, the students mentioned two U.S. presidents known for their tough stands against Communism—Harry S. Truman and Ronald Reagan—and Wladyslaw Sikorski, the leader of Poland's government-in-exile during World War II.

That same year, 1997, Poland passed a completely new constitution to replace the 1952 constitution, written by the Communist government. In 1999 Poland took a major step toward integrating with the West by joining the North Atlantic Treaty Organization (NATO), a military alliance of nations that includes France, Great Britain, Canada, and the United States.

Three years later, Poland completed another major step in this direction when it was invited to join the European Union (EU), an organization that facilitates cooperation among its members in matters of trade, politics, and economics. In 2003 the Polish government demonstrated its commitment to the United States and its support for the global war on terrorism by sending troops to assist in the U.S.-led invasion of Iraq. Following the successful removal of Iraqi dictator Saddam Hussein, Polish troops remained in Iraq to help with the rebuilding of the country and are scheduled to leave the country in 2006.

Government

The 1989 agreement between the Communist government and the Solidarity union restructured the country's legislative bodies. Poland has a bicameral (two-house) legislature known as the National Assembly. The Sejm, or lower house, consists of 460 locally elected representatives. The Senate, or upper house, has one hundred members. The Sejm passes laws and approves government appointments. The Senate reviews—but cannot veto—legislation passed by the Sejm.

Poland's **parliament building** is located in Warsaw. The legislature, which is made up of the Sejm and the Senate, meets here.

The president, who is elected by a popular vote to a five-year term, has broad powers, including the authority to conduct foreign policy and to oversee international security. The president also may veto laws passed by the Sejm, which can then overturn the veto by a two-thirds vote. The president appoints the prime minister, who heads a council of ministers.

The Polish judicial system includes a supreme court, which makes final decisions on cases that come from the lower courts. A constitutional tribunal reviews legislation, and a state tribunal tries high-ranking government officials accused of breaking the law. Provincial courts hear criminal and civil cases, and local courts consider civil matters and minor crimes.

Poland consists of sixteen provinces known as *voivodships*. Each has elected assemblies that control much of the local tax-generated revenue.

THE PEOPLE

From the time of the Piast dynasty until the 1950s, most Poles lived on farms. The few large cities that thrived from Poland's trade—such as Krakow, Warsaw, and Poznan—were home to a multiethnic population of Poles and other northern Europeans, including Germans, Dutch people, and Scandinavians. Before World War II, many Jews, Ukrainians, Czechs, and Belarussians also lived in Poland.

Rapid industrialization and the redrawing of Poland's borders after the war brought about further changes. The Soviet Union annexed a large part of eastern Poland, and most ethnic Germans fled to eastern Germany. New factories drew workers from the countryside, where state collectives forced many farmers off their land. In the twenty-first century, ethnic Poles make up about 97 percent of Poland's population of 38.6 million. The remaining 3 percent are mostly Belarussian, German, or Ukrainian. About two-thirds of the country's people are city dwellers.

Since the end of Communism, the living standard of urban Poles versus rural Poles has become increasingly unequal, as many urbanites have come to enjoy some prosperity while the country's farming areas continue to struggle. A majority of Poles live on the Central Plains, where Warsaw, Lodz, Poznan, and Wroclaw are located. Heavy industries and mines have made Silesia the country's most urbanized region. The Carpathian Forelands, with their fertile land and rich mineral resources, are also heavily populated.

Language

Following the partitions of Poland and the disappearance of the Polish state at the end of the eighteenth century, Poles were pressured to speak the language of their rulers. The Polish language therefore became a key means for Poles to maintain their ethnic identity. In modern times, virtually all Poles speak the Polish language, which is one of the Western Slavic languages, a group that also includes Czech and Slovak. The language uses the Latin alphabet, but a number of diacritical marks are used to reflect differences in pronunciation. For example, the letter *ł* is pronounced like the *w* in the word *wine*. Widespread public education since World War II standardized written and spoken Polish, but regional dialects survive. Silesian dialects, for example, are a mixture of Polish and German. The Gorale people of the Carpathian Mountains also have a distinctive dialect.

German and English are the most commonly spoken non-Polish languages. Many city dwellers—especially those who work in the tourism industry—speak English, German, or both. Some older Poles who live in areas that were once part of Germany remain familiar with the German tongue.

◉ Health

Under Communism, all citizens received free medical treatment at public clinics and hospitals. However, the country's health-care system was chronically underfunded and often struggled to meet the needs of the Polish public. After the end of Communism, the Solidarity government instituted an ambitious plan to reform the country's health-care system by placing responsibility for the health-care sector in the hands of regional governments and by encouraging the opening of more private health clinics. This plan proved ineffective and led to significant reductions of access to health care for many citizens. Hospitals and clinics have experienced severe staff shortages, and hospitals have at times turned away sick patients who could not pay for treatment.

In recent years, the government has continued to work toward the improvement of the health-care system. All adult working citizens pay in to the national health-care system. In return, all citizens are entitled to health care at government hospitals and clinics. Wealthier Poles often pay extra to visit private clinics and hospitals, where care is often superior to government clinics.

Poland's heavy industrialization has led to air and water pollution, especially in the industrial and mining cities of the south. As a result, health problems in the region include high rates of respiratory diseases and cancer. The average life expectancy is slightly less than 73 years. Poland's infant mortality rate—the number of children who die within their first year—is 10 deaths per 1,000 live births. This figure

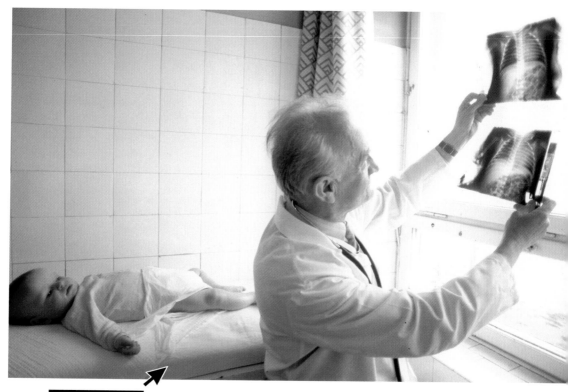

A **doctor in Poland** reviews X-rays of a baby's lungs. Go to www.vgsbooks.com for links to further information about Poland's health system, as well as up-to-date population figures and other statistics.

is significantly higher than Poland's neighbor to the west, Germany (4 deaths per 1,000 live births) but similar to the former Communist nations of Central Europe.

For the most part, Poland has so far avoided the global HIV (human immunodeficiency virus) and AIDS (acquired immunodeficiency syndrome) epidemic. About 8,700 Poles are living with HIV, and about 1,400 have AIDS. Intravenous drug users account for the majority of HIV/AIDS cases, with most occurrences being found in the urban areas of Gdansk, Warsaw, and Katowice. Poland's Ministry of Health recently introduced national programs designed to help prevent HIV infection and to provide care for persons living with HIV/AIDS.

Education

Poles have long considered education important. Polish rulers sought to spread education to their subjects as early as the twelfth century, when experts on agriculture were brought from other parts of Europe to teach Polish peasants the latest farming techniques. In 1364 Casimir the Great founded Krakow University (since renamed Jagiellonian University), which soon became one of Europe's great

This building is part of the **Jagiellonian University** in Krakow. It is the oldest university in Poland.

academic institutions. Later, in 1773, King Stanislaus August created the world's first state ministry of education, the Commission on National Education, which established a uniform national education system that focused on mathematics, natural sciences, and language studies.

During the partition period, ethnic Poles worked to preserve their homeland's national identity through education. As Prussia, Austria, and Russia sought to destroy the Polish identity through "Russification" and "Germanization" programs that forced Poles to learn, speak, and read the language of their foreign rulers, courageous Poles risked prosecution by continuing to teach, write, and publish books in Polish.

Poland's rebirth following World War I saw a renaissance of education, which included the restructuring of the former Austrian, Russian, and Prussian systems into one single Polish system. This period also witnessed the opening of several universities, including schools of higher education in Warsaw and Poznan. The German invasion in 1939 carried with it a plan to wipe out Polish culture altogether. The German occupiers closed all secondary and higher education schools to Poles, and all discussion of Poland as a nation was forbidden in every grade level.

Under Communism, education played a key role in the restructuring of society along Communist lines. The Communist education system closely controlled all school curricula (study programs) and stressed secular (nonreligious) teachings while emphasizing the importance of work and the working class. The few official religious schools that existed were tightly controlled by the Communist government. Public education at all levels was free.

Since the end of Communism, many secondary and higher education schools charge tuition. However, education remains free for the younger grades, and attendance is compulsory from the ages of seven to fifteen. Poland's literacy rate—the percentage of adults who can read and write—is above 99 percent.

Elementary schools—which are in session five hours a day, five days a week—offer special classes and extracurricular activities after regular school hours. Athletic programs include soccer, bicycle racing, track and field, volleyball, and skiing.

After they have completed eighth grade, students may enroll in vocational schools or take an entrance exam for a secondary school of liberal arts. Students who pass this exam spend four years studying

Polish **students** in a public school work on a math lesson. Religion is also a standard classroom subject in Poland.

CULTURAL LIFE

Poland's position as a crossroads between eastern and western Europe has had a profound effect on its people and culture. While the nation's people share their Slavic ancestry with their neighbors to the south and east, over the centuries, Poles also experienced the Western cultural eras of the Renaissance and the Enlightenment that helped shape modern Western thought and art. The result is a Polish culture that values faith but also encourages tolerance.

▶ Religion

Prince Mieszko I brought Christianity to Poland in 966, although the Roman Catholic Church would not become widespread among the population until the 1200s. Since that time, however, the Church has wielded great influence in Poland. Loyalty to the Catholic Church helped Poles maintain their national identity during the era of partition and foreign rule in the 1800s. Later, when the Nazi occupation and then the Communist government

restricted religious practices, some churches and seminaries remained open or operated secretly. Catholic leaders joined the opposition to the regime, and the Polish cardinal Karol Wojtyla, who became Pope John Paul II in 1978 and served until his death in 2005, used his power and popularity to press for reform.

The Roman Catholic Church was instrumental in bringing about the toppling of Poland's Communist regime partly through its support for Solidarity. Since that time, the Church has remained active in politics. In Poland there is far less separation of church and state than is found in other Western countries. Local clergy often openly support political candidates who reflect the Church's doctrine, and the Church leadership has worked tirelessly to guide the passage of laws that banned abortion and made religious instruction mandatory, even in public schools.

More than 95 percent of Poles are Roman Catholic. The remainder are mostly Eastern Orthodox or Protestant Christians.

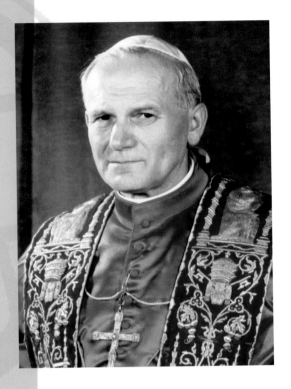

Poland's reputation for religious tolerance attracted many Jews to the country, and before World War II, Poland was home to about 3 million Jews. Most of them were killed during the Holocaust. Following the war, many Holocaust survivors emigrated to Palestine and helped found the State of Israel in 1948. Only 5,000 to 10,000 Jews still live in Poland.

Literature, Media, and Film

Poles take great pride in their literature, which long has been an important expression of their national identity. Poland's first literary works were lyric and epic poems that were sung or spoken. After the nation converted to Christianity, Latin became the dominant language for both secular and religious writing.

By the middle of the fifteenth century, Polish was replacing Latin as the nation's literary language. The sixteenth-century poet Jan Kochanowski (1530–1584) wrote in both Latin and Polish. Mikolaj Rej (1505–1596) earned the title Father of Polish Literature for satires, poems, and prose that he wrote exclusively in Polish. Later Polish writers produced important works of poetry, history, and religion.

Polish literature gained increasing importance during the 1800s. Poets such as Adam Mickiewicz (1798–1855) kept Polish culture and patriotism alive during this period of partition and foreign rule. Mickiewicz's epic poem, *Lord Thaddeus* (1834), expressed his deep love for Poland.

A number of Polish writers have earned the Nobel Prize for Literature. The first among them is Henryk Sienkiewicz, who received the award in 1905 for *Quo Vadis?*, an epic historical novel set during the days of the Roman Empire. In 1924 novelist and short story writer Wladyslaw Reymont (1868–1925) received the same prize for his epic *The Peasants*. Poet Czeslaw Milosz (1911–2004) was awarded the Nobel in 1980 for his works, which explore a wide variety of topics and were often harshly critical of Poland's Communist regime. In 1996 Wislawa Szymborska (b. 1923) received the prize for her poetry.

Milosz is one of many Polish writers who became exiles, living abroad to escape the repressive culture and censorship of Communist rule. He and others have made important contributions to non-Polish cultures as well. Jozef Teodor Konrad Korzeniowski (1857–1924) moved to Britain, where he penned many classic stories in English under the name Joseph Conrad. The best-known of Conrad's works include the novels *Lord Jim* (1900), *The Secret Agent* (1907), and the short novel *Heart of Darkness* (1902). The works of Polish-born Isaac Bashevis Singer (1904–1991) of world-class renown describe traditional Jewish myths and legends. Jerzy Kosinski (1933–1991), like Singer, emigrated to the United States. Among his novels is *The Painted Bird* (1965), a frightening account of the hardships experienced by Poles during World War II.

While in power, Poland's Communist regime placed heavy restrictions on authors. Nevertheless, many Poles continued to publish their works secretly. Since the end of Communist rule, Poland has one of the most active publishing industries in central

Joseph Conrad was born in a part of Poland that later became part of Ukraine. He moved to Great Britain and wrote many classic novels in English.

Europe, with nearly 3,000 magazines and newspapers. Poles buy 200 million books a year, including many that were not available during the Communist era.

The Communist government also strictly controlled the media. Newspapers and news programs created a positive picture of Communism while maintaining a negative perspective on the non-Communist West. Because the media's rosy portrayal of Communism did not reflect reality, the Polish public developed a very cynical attitude toward the media. This attitude persists, despite the fact that the Polish media became free and independent after the fall of the Communist regime.

Poles are avid television watchers, and there are more than 13 million television sets in the country. Although a wide variety of broadcast stations are available, many Poles own satellite dishes, which provide access to programming from parts of Western Europe and from the United States.

Under Communism, radio was a very important media, because television sets were a scarce commodity. In the early 2000s, there are about 20 million radios in Poland. Poles have access to 14 AM radio stations and over 700 FM stations.

The first Polish film was produced in 1908, and since that time, the country has been home to a thriving film industry. The years between 1955 and 1963 were a particularly fruitful period, with a number of masterpieces being made. The leading light of this time was director Andrzej Wajda (b. 1926), who produced a trilogy of films: *Pokolenie (A Generation)* in 1955, *Kanal (Canal)* in 1957, and *Popiol i Diament (Ashes and Diamonds)* in 1958. These three films bring to life the Polish experience during World War II. Wajda has gone on to direct more than thirty films and received an honorary Academy Award for his lifetime of work in 1999. Other well known modern Polish film directors include Agnieszka Holland (b. 1948) and Krzysztof Kieslowski (1941–1996).

Perhaps the most internationally famous Polish film director is Roman Polanski, who made his best and most popular films while working in the United States. Polanski's most famous films are *Rosemary's Baby* (1968), *Chinatown* (1974), and *The Pianist* (2002). The latter film, which tells the story of famed Polish concert pianist Wladyslaw Szpilman's struggle to survive the Holocaust, earned Polanski an Academy Award for Best Director.

 ## Music, Drama, and Art

Poland's folk music has been renowned throughout Europe, and Polish classical composers stayed close to the nation's folk traditions. Many

Frederic Chopin was a famous Polish pianist and composer who lived in the mid-1800s. He died at the young age of thirty-nine.

Polish composers of the nineteenth century wrote versions of the polonaise and the mazurka, Poland's national dances.

Poland's most famous composer, the pianist Frederic Chopin (1810–1849), left Poland to study and perform in France. He based much of his piano music—including polo-naises, mazurkas, and waltzes—on Polish folk rhythms and melodies. Chopin's innovations in classical harmony made him a leading figure of nineteenth-century music.

Like Chopin, Ignace Jan Paderewski (1860–1941) was a celebrated pianist who spent many years outside his homeland. A diplomat as well as a musician, Paderewski served as Poland's prime minister and foreign minister after World War I. Wanda Landowska (1879–1959), a Polish harpsichordist, was renowned for her performances of eighteenth-century music, especially the keyboard works of Johann Sebastian Bach. Karol Szymanowski (1882–1937) and Krzysztof Penderecki (b. 1933) revolutionized concert music with their new approaches to musical harmony and structure.

Modern Poles enjoy many different musical styles, from classical to jazz to rock and roll. Western rock groups have toured in Polish cities, and jazz festivals take place each year in Wroclaw and Krakow.

Drama has been performed in Poland since the Piast dynasty. In the late 1700s, actor, director, and writer Wojciech Boguslawski (1757–1829) pioneered a Polish national theater. The nineteenth-century actress Helena Modrzejewska (1840–1909), who used the stage name Modjeska, performed Shakespearean plays and other dramas in Poland, Western Europe, and the United States.

After World War II, Polish drama was used by the Communist government for political propaganda. The Popular Theater in Nowa Huta and the Dramatic Theater in Warsaw focused on moral and political problems. In the 1960s, student theaters combined the talents of painters, singers, actors, and jazz musicians to produce satirical comedy. These theaters provided a stage for writers whose printed works came under heavy censorship by the Communist regime.

Like Polish musicians, Polish artists flourished during the 1800s. One of the most famous Polish painters, Jan Matejko (1838–1893) of Krakow, produced historical scenes on huge canvases. His most famous painting is *Sobieski Sending Message of Victory to the Pope after the Battle of Vienna* (1880), which portrays Jan Sobieski's victory over the Turks at Vienna in 1683. Matejko also produced a gallery of portraits of more than forty Polish kings. Jozef Chelmonski (1849–1914), a well-known nineteenth-century realist, painted scenes from rural life.

Generations of rural families have kept Polish folk art alive. *Wycinanki*—paper cutouts made with scissors—originated in the 1800s. Common wycinanki designs depict trees, flowers, farm animals, and birds. Traditional folk art also includes rug and tapestry weaving, historic- and religious-themed wood carving, pottery making, and painting on glass.

> To learn more about famed Polish painter Jan Matejko and to see images of some of his works, including his famous Gallery of Polish Kings, visit www.vgsbooks.com for links.

Holidays, Festivals, and Food

Easter and Christmas are the major religious holidays in Poland. Many Polish Catholics observe Lent (the forty days before Easter) by eating little meat or sweets. On Good Friday, the Friday before Easter, devout Poles fast (eat little or no food), and on Easter Sunday, nearly all Catholic Poles attend Easter Mass. This is followed by a festive feast, which often includes a wide variety of foods such as baked ham, sausages, roast beef, salads, and traditional desserts, including *mazurek* and *babkas*.

Christmas is second only to Easter in importance among Poles. Christmas Eve day is marked by fasting and tree decorating. The evening is capped off with a special meal called the Wigilia, which may include as many as twelve courses, ranging from mushroom or fish soup to boiled carp, cabbage and mushrooms, noodles seasoned with poppy seeds, and stewed prunes. Many Polish Catholics attend a midnight Christmas Mass, and Christmas Day is usually spent in the company of relatives.

On Assumption Day, August 15, many Polish Catholics make a pilgrimage to the Jasna Gora Monastery at Czestochowa to honor the shrine of the Black Madonna. Devout Poles believe that this painting of the Virgin Mary and her baby, Jesus, miraculously stopped a

Dancers and musicians in traditional costume celebrate the season at **Dozynki, the Harvest Festival.**

Swedish invasion in the seventeenth century. In modern times, many Poles believe the Black Madonna can perform miracles, and the painting is an important symbol of the Polish nation.

Nonreligious holidays and festivals in Poland include the national holidays Constitution Day (May 3) and Independence Day (November 11), when Poles commemorate the rebirth of their nation following World War I. Most Polish farming communities celebrate the Dozynki (Harvest Festival) with music, dancing, parades, and food.

Polish meals vary according to what is available in each region. Along the Baltic coast, for example, herring is a staple food. Poles living in forested regions gather wild mushrooms and berries. Wild game—including boar, venison, and pheasant—is popular in the Carpathians. Traditional meals may also include locally grown potatoes, beets, cabbage, spinach, apples, pears, currants, and strawberries.

For centuries Poles have eaten cabbage fresh or preserved as sauerkraut. *Golabki* are cooked cabbage leaves stuffed with chopped meat and served with mushroom or tomato sauce. Other common foods are beet soup,

DYNGUS DAY

The Monday following Easter Sunday is known as Dyngus Day in Poland. This holiday features a unique ritual in which boys and young men splash girls and young women with water. The exact origins of this ritual are unclear, but it may originally have been a commemoration of Prince Mieszko's baptism in 966 (Christian baptism involves dousing or touching the person with water), which marked the birth of Christianity in Poland.

ROYAL MAZUREK

These delicious treats are traditionally served at Easter. Orange and lemon give these simple bars a springtime flavor.

Dough:

1 cup (2 sticks) butter, softened

1¼ cup sugar

1 cup finely ground almonds

1 teaspoon vanilla extract

grated rind of one orange, or about 2 tablespoons dried, grated orange peel

5 egg whites

1½ cups all-purpose flour

Icing:

1 cup powdered sugar

2 teaspoons lemon juice

1. Preheat oven to 350°F.
2. Grease and flour a medium cookie sheet.
3. In a large mixing bowl, combine butter and sugar, and beat at high speed for 5 minutes. Add almonds, vanilla extract, and orange rind, and mix well.
4. In a medium mixing bowl, beat egg whites until stiff. Gradually fold flour, then egg whites, into butter and sugar mixture, and mix gently.
5. Spread over cookie sheet and bake for 40 minutes, or until golden brown.
6. While mazurek is cooling, prepare icing by combining powdered sugar and lemon juice. When mazurek is cool, spread icing over top. Cut into small squares and serve.

Makes about 40 squares.

kielbasa (smoked sausage), potatoes, sour cream, rye bread, and beer. Cooks stuff dough with meat, sauerkraut, fresh cabbage, potatoes, and cheese to make pierogi (dumplings). *Bigos*, a popular stew that has many variations, combines meat, cabbage, sauerkraut, and seasonings. Favorite spices include dill, marjoram, and caraway seeds.

Many Poles begin the day with buttered bread and tea or coffee, sometimes accompanied by eggs, sausage, cheese, and ham or other sliced meats. Instead of lunch, Poles eat a second breakfast of bread and butter with cheese, sliced cucumbers, tomatoes, and tea. The late afternoon meal features soup, a meat or fish course, potatoes, vegetables, and a dessert of cakes or tarts. A late evening supper is often similar to breakfast.

Sports and Recreation

Poles enjoy a wide variety of recreational sports. The Carpathian Mountains in the south offer miles of hiking trails, as well as rock climbing, camping, and skiing. The lakes of the north are favorite locations for sailing and water skiing. Canoeists paddle the Czarna Hancza River. A system of 17 national parks has been established in Poland's forests, mountains, and coastal areas.

Soccer, which Europeans call football, is Poland's most popular team sport. The nation takes pride in several outstanding professional soccer teams that draw spectators from across Europe. Basketball is played by amateur teams, and Polish volleyball squads have won gold medals in the Summer Olympic Games.

Poland has produced more than its fair share of world-class athletes over the decades, and Poles have set Olympic records in several sports. During the 1980 games, Wladyslaw Kozakiewicz broke the previous pole vault record and Grazyna Rabsztyn set a new record in the 100-meter hurdles.

Polish athletes carried home a total of 14 medals from the 2000 Summer Olympic Games in Sydney, Australia, in sports ranging from gymnastics to track and field to canoeing to weight lifting. Ski jumper Adam Malysz is perhaps Poland's most popular athlete. Malysz earned a bronze and a silver medal at the 2002 Winter Olympic Games at Salt Lake City, Utah. Polish athletes carried home another ten medals from the 2004 Summer Olympic Games in Athens, Greece. Swimmer Otylia Jedrzejczak became a hero in her country when she won three medals—one gold and two silver—at the Athens games.

Adam Malysz won two medals in the 2002 Winter Olympic Games in ski jumping.

THE ECONOMY

Before World War II, farming was Poland's most important economic activity. About two-thirds of the Polish people lived on farms, and the country was self-sufficient in food. In the decades following the war, the Communist regime imposed a Soviet-style Communist economy that was based on central planning as opposed to supply and demand. The government controlled virtually all aspects of the economy, including wages, prices, and the amount and kinds of goods produced. During this period, the Communist regime focused its efforts on transforming Poland from a farming country into an industrialized nation. The government built new plants to produce steel, chemicals, and textiles and forced many farmers to seek factory jobs in Polish cities.

As the rural population declined, however, half as many farmers bore the burden of feeding Poland's growing urban population. Shortages of food and other items occurred, and living standards fell. Poland had to borrow heavily to keep its industries running and to

import needed goods. Strikes and demonstrations during the 1980s eventually ended Polish Communism and led to the establishment of a free market economy.

By the time the new Solidarity government took power, the Polish economy was in chaos. Poland's gross domestic product (or GDP—the amount of goods and services produced in a country in one year) shrank by 18 percent between 1989 and 1991, industrial output dropped by one-third during this same period, and inflation spiraled at a staggering rate of 30 percent per month. In the midst of these difficulties, the new government instituted a wide range of reforms outlined by the Polish economist Leszek Balcerowicz.

Balcerowicz's plan, which came to be known as Shock Therapy, sought to stabilize the economy while instituting reforms. Privatization and liberalization—removing barriers to foreign trade, private businesses, and market-driven pricing—were the main elements of the reforms.

In the short term, Shock Therapy stabilized inflation, brought an end to central planning, and lifted controls on prices and wages. No longer owned or supported by the state, inefficient firms cut back their operations or went out of business. The result was a sharp rise in unemployment and an even further decline in living standards for some Poles.

Yet, by the mid-1990s, Poland had experienced a dramatic recovery. In 1996 the country became the first formerly Communist country to regain or surpass its 1989 GDP. Since that time, Poland has generally enjoyed steady economic growth, albeit with some fluctuations. Unemployment, however, remains a serious problem—nearly 20 percent of Poles who are capable of work cannot find jobs. Meanwhile, Poland has rapidly transformed its economy from an outdated industry-based model into a more modern, service-based economy. Most economists see Poland's entry into the European Union in 2004 as positive for Poland's economy, as it has encouraged more trade with Western Europe by lowering or eliminating tariffs (taxes) on Polish exports to member nations.

Poland's GDP is about $463 billion. This number places Poland as the twenty-sixth-largest economy in the world, just behind the Netherlands and slightly larger than the Philippines.

COMPARING GDP PER CAPITA

The GDP per capita statistic— GDP divided by a country's population—gives a rough idea of the yearly income and living standards of the average citizen. Poland's GDP per capita (in U.S. dollars) is about $12,000. This ranks 72nd in the world, just behind Argentina and just ahead of Saudi Arabia. For comparison, here is a list of the GDP per capita of some other countries, including some of Poland's neighbors:

Luxembourg (1st)—$58,900
United States (2nd)—$40,100
Canada (15th)—$31,500
Germany (24th)—$28,700
Czech Republic (59th)—$16,800
Slovakia (63rd)—$14,500
Lithuania (70th)—$12,500
Russia (82nd)—$9,800
Belarus (108th)—$6,800
Ukraine (115th)—$6,300
Ethiopia (219th)—$800

Services and Tourism

The service sector is made up of economic activities that provide services rather than goods. Services include retail, banking, insurance, education, and health care. Poland's service sector has expanded rapidly since the end of Communism. Services account for 66 percent of Poland's GDP and employ 55 percent of the workforce. A large part of the sector's expansion has been due to the establishment of numerous small and medium-sized private businesses, such as retail stores, workshops, and restaurants.

More than 14 million people visited Poland in 2004, and this number has been steadily increasing. Although Poland lacks the warm and sunny climate favored by many European travelers, the country boasts historical and cultural treasures, as well as recreational spots and health resorts.

In Krakow tourists can explore the Wawel Cathedral and an impressive historical museum in Wawel Castle. Visitors to the Wieliczka salt mine tour old chambers and view salt statues and chandeliers in the Chapel of the Blessed King. The Castle of the Teutonic Knights at Malbork, near Gdansk, is an impressive, ancient stronghold. The Amber Museum in the castle displays prehistoric plants and insects preserved in ancient amber resin.

Many of Poland's important historical sites date to World War II. A museum at the site of Auschwitz concentration camp, west of Krakow, reminds visitors of the millions who were killed there by the Nazis. Tourists in Warsaw's Castle Square visit the rebuilt statue of King Zygmunt III Vasa, who made Warsaw the Polish capital. The pieces of the original statue, shattered during World War II, are on display nearby.

Ski resorts, such as Zakopane in the Tatra Mountains, draw winter vacationers. The Vistula and other rivers attract canoeists, and the Baltic coast is famous for its mineral water spas. Poland's horse-breeding establishments give tourists an opportunity to enjoy riding tours through the countryside, where many old manor houses and palaces are open for overnight stays. Visitors can also take horse-drawn carriage rides through the Bialowieza Forest.

Located just outside of Gdansk, **Westerplatte Monument** marks the location where World War II started.

Manufacturing, Trade, Mining, and Energy

For most of the Communist era, manufacturing was Poland's most important economic activity. In 1988 industry accounted for almost 42 percent of GDP, but in the early 2000s, this number has dropped to 31 percent. About 29 percent of Poland's workforce is engaged in industry. Under the drive for privatization in the early 1990s, many smaller manufacturing firms and plants were privatized. The government has struggled, however, to find buyers for the country's larger industrial companies, and most of them remain publicly owned.

Poland's chief industrial area is Silesia, a region of heavy manufacturing, mining, and energy production in the southwest. Factories in Warsaw and Krakow make steel, textiles, electronic equipment, and building materials. Gdansk and Gdynia, key Baltic Sea ports, boast large shipbuilding industries. For more than a century, the textile mills at Lodz produced woolen and cotton products for export to Russia. Other major Polish industries manufacture cement, appliances, agricultural fertilizers, and processed foods.

During the 1980s, Poland traded mainly with other Communist nations and with developing countries in the Middle East. Poland's industrialization made it a leading exporter of raw materials and building supplies to these regions. As many Communist countries changed their economic systems in the early 1990s, the Soviet-led trading bloc in Eastern Europe fell apart, and Poland's trade with Western nations increased. This trend has accelerated with Poland's entry into the European Union.

Two women sew upholstery for cars in a **factory** in a town in western Poland. Nearly 98 percent of the factory's products are exported to the European Union.

Minerals, finished metals, and raw materials—such as coal, copper, and sulfur—are important Polish exports, as are machinery and transport equipment, manufactured goods and food. Poland's chief imports are machinery, food, crude oil, cotton, and iron ore. The leading sources of imported goods are Germany, Italy, Russia, France, and the Netherlands. Poland's chief exporting markets are Germany, Italy, France, Great Britain, and the Czech Republic. Poland imports about $5.5 billion more in products than it exports.

Coal is Poland's most important mineral resource. The extensive deposits in Silesia have made this region one of the world's leading exporters of coal, although coal production has dropped since the early 1990s. Fields in southern and southwestern Poland hold an estimated 24 billion tons (about 22 billion metric tons) of both bituminous (hard) coal and lignite (soft) coal. The largest field lies near Katowice, a major mining and metal-processing center.

The Polish Uplands contain reserves of copper, zinc, lead, and sulfur. Although Polish companies mine small amounts of iron ore, the country must import additional iron for its large steel and shipbuilding industries.

A rich supply of rock salt exists in southern and central Poland. The salt mine at Wieliczka, near Krakow, has produced salt for many centuries. Amber, a semiprecious stone, is found in small deposits along the coast of the Baltic Sea. Workshops polish the material and shape it into jewelry.

ENERGY CONSUMPTION IN POLAND

Poland's energy consumption has dropped significantly since the end of the Communist era. Much of the change has been the result of the Polish government closing many inefficient industrial plants. But another key factor has been the government and Polish citizens showing a commitment to energy efficiency. Under Communism the government supplied energy at no charge. Homes and businesses had no incentive to be more energy efficient, and the result was a very wasteful use of energy. For example, turning up the heat and leaving windows open in winter was not an uncommon practice under Communism. Few homes or buildings were insulated, and few had thermostats that could regulate indoor temperatures for maximum efficiency. Since 1989 the Polish government has worked extensively to educate the Polish population about energy efficiency and has also modernized many buildings to make them more energy efficient.

A miner stands beside an enormous extractor machine at a **mine** in Belchatow in central Poland.

The oil fields of Poland stretch across 9,000 square miles (23,300 sq. km) in the foothills of the Carpathian Mountains. Poland has about 96 million barrels of proven oil reserves. The supply of domestic crude oil, however, cannot meet the demand created by the country's factories, homes, and motor vehicles. As a result, Poland must import 95 percent of its oil. Power plants that burn hard coal and lignite generate most of the nation's electricity. Hydroelectric plants on the Vistula River and along other waterways supply additional power.

Agriculture, Forestry, and Fishing

Agriculture accounts for just 3 percent of Poland's GDP but employs 16 percent of the country's workforce. After World War II, Poland's government organized many private farms into state-owned collective farms. Farmers on the collectives shared their labor and equipment. The government paid a fixed wage and required the collectives to sell all of their produce to the state. By the 1950s, nearly half of Poland's land had been collectivized.

At the end of the 1950s, however, the collective-farm system was failing. Because they did not own their equipment, hired farmers had little incentive to take proper care of agricultural machinery. Because they earned fixed wages, farmers also lacked incentive to produce bigger harvests. To profit in a black market for food, some farmers underreported their harvests and kept produce to sell privately. The food shortages that resulted from these practices led the government to return Polish farms to private ownership, although the state still controlled the use of fertilizers and machinery.

In the 2000s, about 2 million family farms exist in Poland. The majority of these farms are small plots of land, ranging from 5 to 12 acres (2 to 5 hectares) in size. About half of Poland's farmers engage in subsistence agriculture—meaning they are only able to grow food for themselves and their family with little or nothing left over to sell for profit. Because the costs of fertilizers, pesticides, and energy are high, many of these farmers do not use chemicals or modern machinery to cultivate their crops.

Poland's most important crops are grains such as wheat, rye, oats, and barley, which are processed for livestock feed, for domestic food markets, or for alcoholic beverages. Rapeseed, used for feeding sheep and pigs, is also made into oil. The vast Central Plains, the fertile Polish Uplands, and the Carpathian Forelands produce most of Poland's grain. These regions also yield vegetable crops, including potatoes and sugar beets. The raising of livestock, especially cattle and sheep, is important in southern Poland.

About 30 percent of Poland is covered by forests, mostly of pine, spruce, and other evergreens. Sawmills in the Lake Region and in the Carpathian Mountains cut about 32 million cubic yards (25 million cubic meters) of wood every year for

Farmers gather **hay** that will be used for feeding livestock.

pulp to make paper and paper products. Mills also process lumber for use in new construction and for mine shaft supports.

Poland's fishing industry—which includes both private individuals and large commercial companies—takes in about 347,000 tons (315,000 metric tons) of fish annually. Small fishing ports, including Darlowo and Ustka, line the Baltic coast, processing herring and cod from the Baltic and North seas and from the open waters of the North Atlantic Ocean.

Transportation

Poland's transportation network includes road, rail, air, and inland shipping systems. Although this network links nearly all of the country's cities and regions, much of the country's roads, highways, and transport equipment is obsolete. Repair and improvements are especially needed on Poland's roads and highways.

Poland's railroads, which were developed in the years before World War I, are the most reliable and common means of shipping goods on land. Poland's railroads run on 14,820 miles (23,852 km) of track. Railroads link cities, ports, and many of the larger towns.

Poland's 226,612 miles (364,697 km) of roads include several important trans-European routes. The inadequacy of Poland's highway system has become a serious problem, as millions of additional cars have choked the country's roads. While about two-thirds of this system is paved, most roads are single-lane highways, and only a small portion of the highway system qualifies as expressways designed to handle heavy traffic. To address this problem, the Polish government

This train is part of the **Polish State Railways** system.

has a $35 billion plan to add more than 93,000 miles (150,000 km) of new roads, including 1,800 miles (3,000 km) of expressways.

The country's rivers and sea-coast have been important for transportation and trade since early times. A system of canals connects waterways and inland ports, including Warsaw and Wroclaw. Barges and small freighters ply the Vistula and Oder rivers. Ships carry coal to the port of Szczecin along the Oder, which is linked by the Gliwice Canal to the industrial and mining centers of Silesia. International shipping moves through the Baltic ports of Gdansk, Gdynia, and Szczecin.

MOBILE PHONES

The mobile phone business is booming in Poland. The country has more mobile phones—17.4 million—in service than regular landlines—12.3 million. Part of the reason for this trend is that the old Communist phone system is in poor condition and badly in need of modernization. In addition, long waits for new landline service have led many Poles to turn to mobile phones.

LOT, the national airline, has both international and domestic flights. It serves Warsaw—the site of Poland's largest international airport—and five other Polish cities.

The Future

The Polish people suffered greatly in the nineteenth and twentieth centuries. After enduring decades of foreign rule, two brutal world wars, more than forty years of Communist mismanagement, and the Shock Therapy of the post-Communist era, Poles are looking forward to a peaceful and prosperous future.

While the process of transforming the country's economy into a free market model has caused a great deal of hardship and produced a backlash against the country's political leaders, the vast majority of Poles realize that these changes are necessary and will lead to a higher standard of living for Poles in the future. For a country that has endured so much trauma with courage and strength, such a future will be well deserved.

Timeline

CA. 13,000 B.C. Prehistoric peoples begin forming communities in the river valleys of modern-day Poland.

CA. 200–500 A.D. Western Slavs, including the Polanie, are inhabiting the area that later becomes Poland.

966 Prince Mieszko I of the Piast dynasty establishes his capital at Gniezno.

1025 The Roman Catholic pope crowns Boleslaus I as king of Poland. Poles adopt the Latin alphabet.

1079 Boleslaus II orders the murder of Bishop Stanislaw of Krakow, an act that angers Polish nobles. Stanislaw flees to Hungary.

1240 Mongolian Tatars invade Poland, causing great destruction.

1320 The Roman Catholic pope crowns Ladislas I king of Poland. Ladislas makes Krakow the new capital of his kingdom.

1333 Casimir III, later known as Casimir the Great, ascends to the throne.

1364 Casimir founds the kingdom's first university, Krakow University (modern-day Jagiellonian University).

1386 Polish nobles elect the Lithuanian duke Jogaila as King Wladislaw II Jagiello, creating a union between Poland and Lithuania.

1410 Polish and Lithuanian forces defeat the Teutonic Knights at the Battle of Tannenberg.

1473 Polish astronomer Mikolaj Kopernik (also known as Copernicus) is born.

1493 Polish nobles form a national parliament, which includes a senate of wealthy nobles and a Sejm, or lower house, of landowners.

1505 The Polish parliament writes the nation's first constitution, which limits the powers of the king.

CA. 1520 Polish printers produce the first Polish-language books.

1569 Poland and Lithuania formally unite under Polish rule.

1683 King Jan III of Poland defeats the Turks in a battle at Vienna, Austria.

1772 Prussia, Russia, and Austria annex a large portion of Polish land in the first partition of Poland.

1795 Prussia, Russia, and Austria seize what remains of Polish land in the third partition of Poland. Poland ceases to exist as an independent nation.

1800s Ethnic Poles struggle to retain their national identity under foreign rule.

1911   Polish scientist Marie Curie wins a Nobel Prize in Chemistry.

1918   A new and independent Poland emerges from the aftermath of World War I (1914-1918).

1920   Poland attacks Russia and expands its territory to the east.

1923   Polish leaders found the Baltic seaport of Gdynia.

1939   Germany and the Soviet Union sign the Molotov-Ribbentrop Pact, in which the two countries agree to divide Poland's territory. Germany invades Poland on September 1, touching off World War II (1939-1945). Soviet forces occupy eastern Poland.

1945   Germany surrenders. Soviet troops occupy Poland. Soviet dictator Joseph Stalin begins to set up a pro-Soviet Communist government in Poland.

1950s   Poland's Soviet-controlled government transforms Poland into an industrial nation.

1956   Violent antigovernment riots break out in Poznan.

1960s   As living standards plummet, Poland's Communist regime becomes increasingly unpopular.

1978   Polish cardinal Karol Wojtyla is elected Pope John Paul II.

1979   Pope John Paul II visits Poland. His trip encourages Poland's anti-Communist leaders to press for changes in government.

1980   A nationwide strike paralyzes Poland and forces the Communist government to negotiate with the country's workers. Workers form the Solidarity trade union. Membership soon swells to ten million.

1981   The Polish government cracks down on opposition by imposing martial law. Solidarity is outlawed.

1983   Pope John Paul II makes a second visit to Poland, bringing the world's attention to the country's plight. Lech Walesa receives the Nobel Peace Prize.

1989   Solidarity is legalized and goes on to win many seats in free and open elections. Communist rule comes to an end.

1990   Lech Walesa becomes the first freely elected president of Poland.

1990s   Poland struggles through its Shock Therapy transformation from a Communist state into a free market economy.

1999   Poland becomes a member of the North American Treaty Organization (NATO).

2003   Polish troops participate in the U.S.-led invasion of Iraq.

2004   Poland officially becomes a member of the European Union on May 1.

2005   Poles mourn the death of Pope John Paul II.

Currency Fast Facts

COUNTRY NAME Republic of Poland

AREA 120,728 square miles (312,685 sq. km)

MAIN LANDFORMS Carpathian Forelands, Central Plains, Coastal Lowlands, Lake Region, Polish Uplands, Sudeten Mountains

HIGHEST POINT Rysy Peak, 8,199 feet (2,499 m) above sea level

LOWEST POINT near Raczki Elblaskie, 6 feet (2 m) below sea level

MAJOR RIVERS Bug, Nysa, Oder, Vistula, Warta

ANIMALS bears, bison, elks, foxes, lynxes, mountain deer, tarpans, wild boars, wolves

CAPITAL CITY Warsaw

OTHER MAJOR CITIES Krakow, Wroclaw, Lodz, Gdansk

OFFICIAL LANGUAGE Polish

MONETARY UNIT Zloty (zl). 100 groszy = 1 zloty

POLISH CURRENCY

The Polish currency is the zloty (pronounced "zwo-ti"), which means "golden." Zloty can be divided into 100 groszy. New notes and coins were introduced in 1995, with five paper bills (10, 20, 50, 100, and 200 zl) and six grosz coins (1, 2, 5, 10, 20, 50 gr) and 3 zloty coins (1, 2, and 5 zl). The bills range in color from blue to yellow to orange, and each bill features a different Polish king on its face. Poland's membership in the EU means that the country will adopt the EU currency, the euro, at some point in the future.

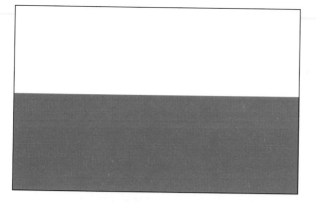

Poland's flag consists of a white horizontal band over a red horizontal band of equal width. The red and white were the colors of the coat of arms of the old Polish-Lithuanian kingdom. The flag was adopted by the Polish legislature in 1919.

The Polish national anthem is "Mazurek Dabrowskiego," or "Dabrowski's Mazurek." A mazurek is a Polish folk dance. The song was written in 1797 by composer Jozef Wybicki and was originally titled "Song of the Polish Legions in Italy." (Henryk Dabrowski was a leader of Polish legions, which fought in Italy at that time.) Over the decades, the song became a rallying cry for Poles who suffered under foreign rulers. It was adopted as the national anthem in 1927. The anthum includes these two verses separated by the chorus.

Poland has not yet perished,
as long as we live.
Whatever foreign force took from us,
we'll retake by sabre.

March, March, Dabrowski,
from Italian land to Poland.
Under your lead,
we'll unite with the nation.

We'll cross Vistula, we'll cross Warta,
We'll be Polish people.
Bonaparte showed us an example
how we should win.

For a link to a site where you can listen to Poland's national anthem, "Mazurek Dabrowskiego," visit www.vgsbooks.com.

CASIMIR THE GREAT (1310–1370) The only Polish monarch to earn the title the Great, Casimir III was born in Kujavia. After inheriting the throne at the age of twenty-three, he quickly showed himself to be a skilled negotiator and administrator. Through a series of treaties, Casimir greatly expanded the size of his kingdom, while strengthening its defenses through the building of dozens of castles in strategic locations. He also codified the kingdom's laws, promoted education and the arts, and fostered economic development through the creation of a stable currency.

FREDERIC CHOPIN (1810–1849) Fryderyk Franciszek Szopen, Poland's greatest composer was born in Zelazowa Wola near Warsaw. Son of a French music teacher, the young Frederic showed a gift for music at a very young age, making his first public performance at the age of eight. The vast majority of his work was written for piano, and he drew much of his inspiration from Polish folk music. By the time he reached his thirties, he was producing some of his greatest works, including *Fantasy in F Minor* (1840–41), the *Barcarolle* (1845–46), the *Polonaise-Fantaisie* (1845–46), *Ballade in F Minor* (1842), and the *Sonata in B Minor* (1844). He died of tuberculosis, an infectious disease that mainly affects the lungs.

COPERNICUS (1473–1543) The astronomer was born Mikolaj Kopernik in Torun in northern Poland. Copernicus's greatest contribution to science was his theory that the earth and the planets revolve around the sun. This contradicted what was then the commonly held belief that the sun and the planets revolve around the earth.

MARIE CURIE (1867–1934) One of history's greatest scientists and the winner of two Nobel prizes, she was born Maria Sklodowska in Warsaw. A brilliant student, she traveled to Paris in her early twenties, where she studied with some of the period's greatest physicists, including Frenchman Pierre Curie, whom she married in 1895. The Curies went on to make many discoveries in the field of radioactivity, including the discovery of the elements polonium (which Marie named after her homeland) and radium. In 1903 Marie, her husband, and fellow French physicist Henri Becquerel were honored for their work with the Nobel Prize in Physics. Eight years later, she received the Nobel Prize in Chemistry.

JOHN PAUL II (1920–2005) The first Polish pope was born Karol Jozef Wojtyla in Watowice. The son of a Polish army officer, he was a student at Jagiellonian University when the Germans invaded Poland in 1939. After witnessing the horrors of the German occupation, he decided to join the Catholic priesthood as a way to help others. He was ordained in 1946 and soon established a reputation as an energetic and thoughtful priest who quietly defied the Communist authorities. He rose steadily through the ranks of the Catholic hierarchy and was named cardinal archbishop of Krakow in 1967. In this position, he used his power to challenge the Communist government. In 1978 he was elected Pope John Paul II. During his tenure as pope, he reached out to other religions and made dozens of visits to foreign countries, in the process, becoming one of the most beloved popes in history.

CZESLAW MILOSZ (1911–2004) Born in Sateiniai, Lithuania, Milosz was one of Poland's greatest poets. In 1933 he published his first book of poetry, *Poemat o czasie zastyglym* (Poem of Frozen Time), in which he expresses fear of an impending, catastrophic war. By the end of the decade, his fears had proven correct. During World War II, he lived in Warsaw, where he actively opposed the Nazi occupation of the city as a member of the Polish resistance. An opponent of the Polish Communist regime, he moved to Paris in 1951 before settling in the United States in 1960. He continued to write poetry and essays—much of it critical of his homeland's Communist government—while teaching Slavic languages and literature at the University of California at Berkeley until he retired in 1980. He was awarded the Nobel Prize for Literature that same year.

IRENA SZEWINSKA (b. 1946) Szewinska is one of Poland's greatest Olympic athletes. She was born Irena Kirszenstein to Polish parents living in Leningrad (modern-day Saint Petersburg), Russia. One of the fastest woman middle-distance runners in history, she made her first Olympic appearance at the 1964 Tokyo Games at the age of eighteen, where she won medals in the long jump, 200-meter race, and as part of the winning 4x100-meter relay team. Szewinska went on to win two medals (bronze in the 100-meter and gold in the 200-meter) at the 1968 Mexico City Games and bronze in the 200-meter at the 1972 Munich Games. At the 1976 Montreal Games, she set a world record while winning the gold in the 400-meter race.

LECH WALESA (b. 1943) The leader of the Solidarity trade union and Poland's first directly elected president was born in Popowo. The son of a carpenter, he worked as an electrician at the Lenin Shipyards at Gdansk, where he soon became a leader of antigovernment activists. After being fired for his activities in 1976, he remained an activist and earned nationwide fame when he climbed the shipyard gates to join striking workers in 1980. Months later, he was chosen to head the new, ten-million-strong Solidarity trade union, which challenged the Communist regime throughout the 1980s. For his attempts to bring about peaceful change in Poland, he was awarded the Nobel Peace Prize in 1983. Walesa was elected the first president of post-Communist Poland in 1990 but failed to win reelection in 1995.

AUSCHWITZ AND BIRKENAU Located about 1 mile (2 km) apart near the city of Oswiecim in southern Poland, Auschwitz and Birkenau are the two most famous World War II Nazi death camps, where about 1.5 million people—most of them Jews—were systematically murdered. The remains of these camps have been converted into museums, in which the visitor can glimpse the horrors of Adolf Hitler's Final Solution, including the giant gas chambers where thousands at a time were murdered and the huge ovens where Nazi executioners cremated the bodies. At Birkenau the ashes of hundreds of thousands of victims were dumped into a nearby pond, giving the water a haunting gray color.

KRAKOW Poland's oldest city was spared from destruction during World War II and is home to about six thousand historic buildings and more than two million works of art. The city's most popular attraction is Wawel Castle, the seat of Poland's kings for more than five hundred years, and Wawel Cathedral, the burial place of most of the nation's kings. Other great sights to see include the dozens of medieval churches and buildings of the city's Old Town. Krakow is also home to one of Europe's finest collections of museums.

SLOWINSKI NATIONAL PARK Located on the Baltic coast west of Gdansk, this 72-square-mile (186 sq. km) park features a variety of plant and animal habitats, including forests, lakes, peat bogs, meadows, and white sand dunes. The latter are a striking sight and give the coastline a desertlike look. The sand is dumped ashore by the water, and after the sand dries, it is carried inland by the wind at a rate of about 6 to 30 feet (2 to 10 m) each year.

WARSAW Poland's capital is a bustling city, full of museums, theaters, shops, bazaars, and excellent restaurants. Almost completely destroyed during World War II, Warsaw's historic sections were meticulously rebuilt using old photographs, drawings, and other resources. Highlights for tourists include the Royal Castle, the seat of the king and the Sejm during the pre-partition period; the rebuilt Old Town with its colorful buildings and shops; the beautiful gardens and architecture of Wilanow Palace and Park; and the National Museum, which features a stunning array of art and artifacts dating from ancient times to the modern age.

WIELICZKA SALT MINES Located just outside of Krakow, this salt mine has been operating for more than seven hundred years. Its maze of tunnels and chambers total almost 200 miles (300 km). A large section of the mines has been preserved as a museum, which is among the most popular tourist attractions in the entire country. This area features numerous statues and artifacts—all carved out of salt—and one of the chambers has even been converted into a beautiful chapel, with altars, chandeliers, and other objects made entirely out of salt.

canal: a human-made waterway

collective farm: a large agricultural estate worked by a group. The workers usually received a portion of the farm's harvest as wages. On a Polish collective farm, the central government owned the land, buildings, and machinery.

Communism: an economic and political system that features government control of businesses and the economy and government rather than private ownership of property

democracy: a government run by the people. In most democracies, citizens control the government by voting for lawmakers and other government officials.

free market economy: a system that allows the free exchange of goods at prices determined by supply and demand

grody: fortified towns

gross domestic product (GDP): a measure of the total value of goods and services produced within a country in a year. A similar measurement is gross national product (GNP). GDP and GNP are often measured in terms of purchasing power parity (PPP). PPP converts values to international dollars, making it possible to compare how much similar goods and services cost to the residents of different countries.

industrialization: the shift from an economy based on farming to one based on manufacturing and industry

Molotov-Ribbentrop Pact: a political agreement negotiated by Vyacheslav Molotov of the Soviet Union and Joachim von Ribbentrop of Germany. Signed in 1939, the agreement said that the two nations would not attack each other or interfere with each other's military and political activities. Germany broke the pact in 1941.

monarchy: a government headed by a leader such as a king, queen, or prince, with titles passed down in the family through generations. Some monarchs hold complete power, while others share their power with other government officials.

moraine: an accumulation of earth and stones carried and deposited by a glacier

pass: a low place in a mountain range

peasant: a small landowner or landless farmworker

privatization: the sale of government-owned businesses to private interests

Roman Catholic Church: a branch of Christianity headed by the pope and based in Vatican City in Rome, Italy. Roman Catholicism is characterized by ceremony, ritual, and reverence for the Virgin Mary and saints, as well as Jesus.

serf: a rural worker under the feudal landowning system, which tied laborers to a farming estate for life. Serfs had few rights and owed their labor and a large portion of their harvest to the landowner.

Slav: a member of an ethnic group that originated in central Asia and later moved into Russia, Ukraine, and eastern Europe

Selected Bibliography

Banaszak, Dariusz, et al. *An Illustrated History of Poland.* Poznan, Poland: Publicat S.A., 2004.
Packed with photos, illustrations, maps, and much more, this colorful and informative book provides a fascinating visual history of Poland.

BBC (British Broadcasting Corporation) News Online. 2005.
http://news.bbc.co.uk/2/hi/europe/default.stm (July 26, 2005).
The BBC's Europe section is a helpful resource for news on Poland and other European nations.

Central Intelligence Agency (CIA). 2005.
http://www.cia.gov/cia/publications/factbook/geos/pl.html (July 26, 2005).
The "World Factbook" section of the CIA's website contains basic information on Poland's geography, people, economy, government, communications, transportation, military, and transnational issues.

Curtis, Glenn E. *Poland: A Country Study.* 3rd ed. Washington, DC: Library of Congress Federal Research Division, 1994.
This volume in the Library of Congress's Area Handbook series provides a wealth of objective information on Poland's history, society, culture, economy, military, and more.

Davies, Norman. *Heart of Europe: The Past in Poland's Present.* 3rd ed. New York: Oxford University Press, 2001.
In this engaging study, noted European history scholar Norman Davies explores the history of Poland by beginning with the present day and working backwards to the Middle Ages.

Dydynski, Krzysztof. *Poland.* 4th ed. Oakland, CA: Lonely Planet Publications, 2002.
This volume in the Lonely Planet Travel Guide series provides up-to-date information for tourists, as well as brief and engaging background essays on the country's geography, people, history, culture, economy, and much more.

The Economist. 2005.
http://www.economist.com (July 26, 2005).
Both the website and print edition of this weekly British news magazine provide up-to-date coverage of Polish news and events.

Griffiths, Clare, et al. *Insight Guide: Poland.* New York: Langenscheidt Publishers, Inc., 2000.
Packed with colorful photos, this volume from Discovery Channel's Insight Guide series provides a wealth of information on Poland's history, people, culture, and arts.

Lukowski, Jerzy, and Hubert Zawadzki. *A Concise History of Poland.* New York: Cambridge University Press, 2001.
Written by two noted Polish historians, this book provides a concise and readable history of the country from its earliest history to the present.

Omilanowska, Malgorzata, et. al. *Warsaw.* **New York: DK Publishing, Inc., 1997.**
Full of detailed maps and hundreds of colorful photos, this volume in the DK Eyewitness Travel Guides series brings Poland's capital to life and features suggested walking tours of the city's most popular tourist destinations.

Population Reference Bureau. **2005.**
http://www.prb.org/ (July 26, 2005).
The annual statistics on this site provide a wealth of data on Poland's population, birth and death rates, fertility rate, infant mortality rate, and other useful demographic information.

Prazmowska, Anita J. *A History of Poland.* **New York: Palgrave Macmillan, 2004.**
Written by a Polish-born professor, this book provides a concise history of Poland from the country's early years to the present.

U.S. Department of State. *Background Notes: Poland.* **2005.**
http://www.state.gov/r/pa/ei/bgn/2875 htm (July 26, 2005).
The U.S. Department of State's website provides basic information such as population statistics, a brief history, analysis of political conditions, and an economic overview of every country in the world, including Poland.

Zamoyski, Adam. *The Polish Way: A Thousand-Year History of the Poles and Their Culture.* **New York: Hippocrene Books, Inc., 1994.**
This is an engaging and well-written history of Poland from the country's earliest history to the anti-Communist strife of the 1980s.

Behnke, Alison. *Pope John Paul II*. Minneapolis: Lerner Publications Company, 2005.
Learn more about the extraordinary life and career of the first Polish-born pope from this volume.

Conrad, Joseph. *Lord Jim*. New York: Penguin Books, 1988.
Joseph Conrad's greatest novel, first published in 1900, tells the story of a young sailor who is forced to stand trial for a crime he didn't commit.

Goldstein, Margaret J. *World War II—Europe*. Minneapolis: Lerner Publications Company, 2004.
This volume in Lerner's Chronicles of America's Wars series explores the events that occurred in the European Theater of World War II and includes information on the invasion of Poland and the Nazi-engineered Holocaust that killed millions of Poles.

Hintz, Martin. *Poland*. New York: Children's Press, 1998.
The Poland volume of the Enchantment of the World series discusses the country's history, culture, land, economy, people, and more.

Jan Matejko
http://artyzm.com/matejko/e_matejko.htm
This site features a large library of images of some of the most famous works of Poland's greatest historical painter, including Matejko's Gallery of Polish Kings.

Morek, Jan, and Olgierd Budrewicz. *Poland*. Warsaw: Wydawnictwa Artystyczne i Filmowe, 2000.
This stunning photo book takes the reader on a journey through Poland's cities and rural areas.

Otfinoski, Steven. *Poland*. New York: Facts on File, 1995.
This volume in the Nations in Transition series provides a brief overview of Poland's land, history, government, people, culture, and economy.

Poland.pl
http://www.poland.pl/
This website provides news reports, links to other Polish sites, and a wealth of other information about Poland, its people, and its culture.

Polish Internet: Polonia: Polish Community around the World
http://www.polskiinternet.com/english/index.html
This helpful website provides links and information about Poland's culture and heritage.

The Sejm of the Republic of Poland
http://www.sejm.gov.pl/english.html (May 23, 2005)
Learn more about Poland's legislature from the Sejm's website.

Serrallier, Ian. *Escape from Warsaw*. New York: Scholastic Paperbacks, 1990.
This is a reprint of Serrallier's classic novel, originally title *The Silver Sword*. Based on a true story, it follows the harrowing journey of a family of five Poles who were separated during World War II and the many adventures they encounter in trying to reunite in Switzerland.

Sherman, Josepha. *The Cold War.* **Minneapolis: Lerner Publications Company, 2004.**
This volume in Lerner's Chronicles of America's Wars series explores the Cold War, the conflict that pitted the United States and its Western European allies against the Soviet Union, Poland, and its Eastern European allies.

Singer, Isaac Bashevis. *When Shlemiel Went to Warsaw and Other Stories.* **New York: Farrar, Straus and Giroux, 1986.**
Famed Polish author Isaac Bashevis Singer retells eight stories of humor and imagination from the lost world of Polish Jewish culture.

vgsbooks.com
http://www.vgsbooks.com
Visit vgsbooks.com, the home page of the Visual Geography Series®. You can get linked to all sorts of useful online information, including geographical, historical, demographic, cultural, and economic websites. The vgsbooks.com site is a great resource for late-breaking news and statistics.

Warsaw Voice
http://www.warsawvoice.pl/
The online version of Poland's oldest and most-respected English-language periodical features news, entertainment reviews, and much, much more.

Zamojska-Hutchins, Danuta. *Cooking the Polish Way.* **Minneapolis: Lerner Publications Company, 2002.**
This volume in Lerner's Easy Menu Ethnic Cookbooks series is full of delicious recipes and useful information about Polish cuisine and culture.

Captions for photos appearing on cover and chapter openers:

Cover: The sunrise casts a pink glow over Saint Mary's Cathedral in the center of Gdansk, Poland.

pp. 4–5 Warsaw's Old Town Square was destroyed, along with most of the city, during World War II. The Polish people rebuilt the entire Old Town.

pp. 8–9 These lakes are in northeastern Poland.

pp. 38–39 Polish children perform a traditional Polish dance.

pp. 46–47 A priest leads a mass at the main alter of Saint Mary's Cathedral. The vast majority of Polish people belong to the Roman Catholic religion.

pp. 56–57 Shipping is an important industry in Poland. These cranes are in the shipyards of Gdansk.

Photo Acknowledgments
The images in this book are used with permission of: © John R. Kreul/Independent Picture Service, pp. 4–5; XNR Productions, pp. 6, 11; © age fotostock/SuperStock, pp. 8–9, 10, 16, 56–57; © Raymond Gehman/CORBIS, p. 14; © Simon Fraser/ Photo Researchers, Inc., p.15; Courtesy Wayne Zuehlke, pp. 18, 42, 44; Courtesy Marta Johnson, pp. 19, 59; Library of Congress, pp. 23 (LC-DIG-ppmsca-00972), 26 (LC-USZ62-85012), 49 (LC-USZ62-47129), 51 (LC-USZ62-103898); *The Illustrated London News*, p. 30; © Bettmann/CORBIS, pp. 31, 48; © United States Holocaust Memorial Museum, p. 32; The Nobel Foundation, p. 34; © Jerzy Dabrowski/ZUMA Press, p. 36; © Zenon Harasym/Art Directors, pp. 38–39; © Giansanti Gianni/CORBIS SYGMA, p. 41; © Getty Images, p. 43; © Steve Raymer/ CORBIS, pp. 46–47; © János Kalmár, p. 53; © Ronald Wittek/Action Press/ZUMA Press, p. 55; © Katarina Stoltz/Reuters/CORBIS, p. 60; © Max Hureau/CORBIS, p. 62; © Warren Jacobs/Art Directors, pp. 62–63 (bottom); © Colin Garratt; Milepost 92½/CORBIS, p. 64; © Independent Picture Service, p. 68.

Cover: © Steve Raymer/CORBIS. Back cover: NASA.